WRITERS AND THEIR WORK

General Editor
ISOBEL ARMSTRONG

Advisory
BRYAN LOUGHREY

Library

CHESTER COLLEGE

JOHN DONNE

from a portrait by an unknown artist c. 1595 reproduced
by permission of the Marquis of Lothian

WWV

John Donne

Stevie Davies

Northcote House
in association with
The British Council

© Copyright 1994 by Stevie Davies

First published in 1994 by Northcote House Publishers Ltd, Plymbridge House, Estover Road, Plymouth PL6 7PZ, United Kingdom. Tel: Plymouth (0752) 735251. Fax: (0752) 695699. Telex: 45635.

British Library Cataloguing-in-Publication Data
A catalogue record for this book is available from the British Library

ISBN 0 7463 0738 1

Typeset by PDQ Typesetting, Stoke-on-Trent
Printed and bound in the United Kingdom by BPC Wheatons Ltd, Exeter

Contents

For Leon Stoger,
the exceptional reader

Acknowledgements

I must thank Frank Regan for his caring support and practical help during the writing of this book, and my friends Margaret Argyle and Ann Mackay for their daily encouragement. A class on Metaphysical Poetry which I led in the Extra-Mural Department at Manchester University was an abundant source of ideas and lines of thought: I should especially thank Simmel Goldberg for the lightning flashes of his epigrammatic wit. I also thank Beth Brownhill, Ruth Smith, Avril Ravenscroft, Andrew Howdle, Monica Davies, Katherine Spearman, Irene Tayler, Pat Shaw, Barbara Cockburn, and Lawrence Tebbott for all their support.

Biographical Outline

John Donne was born in 1572, the son of a London ironmonger. His family was staunchly Roman Catholic, related to Sir Thomas More, the 'Catholic martyr', and to the recusant Heywood family. He was educated at Oxford and Cambridge universities, leaving before he could take a degree, and went on to Lincoln's Inn. Donne sailed in the two expeditions of Lord Essex to Cadiz and the Islands, in 1596 and 1597. His conversion from Catholicism was a gradual process, compounded of genuine soul-searching adulterated perhaps with place-seeking. As secretary to Sir Thomas Egerton, Keeper of the Great Seal, from 1598 to 1602, Donne's ambitions for high office seemed set for fulfilment, but his clandestine marriage to Ann More, niece of the Lord Keeper's wife, blighted his prospects of secular promotion. He lived in the political wilderness for at least a decade, mainly in Mitcham. In 1615 he yielded to King James's pressure to accept ecclesiastical preferment and took holy orders, rising swiftly to become Dean of St Paul's in 1621. He died in 1631.

Abbreviations and References

Texts have been chosen with an eye to their accessibility to the general reader. H. J. C. Grierson's edition of *Donne: Poetical Works* (Oxford, 1979) has been used throughout in quoting Donne's poetry, but checked against other editions (see Select Bibliography).

The following abbreviations have been used in citing key works:

Bald	R. C. Bald, *John Donne: A Life* (Oxford, 1970)
Carey	J. Carey, *John Donne: Life, Mind and Art* (London, 1981)
Casebook	J. Lovelock (ed.), *Donne's 'Songs and Sonets': A Casebook* (London and Basingstoke, 1973)
Heritage	A. J. Smith (ed.), *John Donne: The Critical Heritage* (London and Boston, 1975)
Sermons	G. R. Potter and E. M. Simpson (eds.), *The Sermons of John Donne*, 10 vols. (Berkeley and Los Angeles, Calif., 1953-62)

1

The Person

The language of John Donne's poetry is provocatively unique. Its singularity tempts readers to imagine that our minds are in touch and tune with an extraordinary individual, whose speech-rhythms and tone of voice can be heard in a more than abstract way, as if they rose off the page as sound-waves, to resonate in the body's as well as the mind's ear. This impression is reinforced by the dramatic situations in which the language is rooted, generating the sense of an immediate moment in a continuum of time. The blank spaces on the page before and after the event of the poem seem like a cover of white silence over the activities and circumstances which initiated and will flow out of the speech-act. We people these silent spaces with inferences deduced from the poem and in our mind's eye glimpse the shadowy 'she' or 'thou' of the woman or man addressed as a fugitive presence just beyond the margin of the book:

> I wonder by my troth, what thou, and I
> Did, till we loved? . . .

> ('The good-morrow', ll. 1–2)

> Stand still, and I will read to thee . . .

> ('A Lecture upon the Shadow', l.1)

> Busie old foole, unruly Sunne . . .

> ('The Sunne Rising', l.1)

> For Godsake hold your tongue, and let me love . . .

> ('The Canonization,' l.1)

Colloquial spontaneity salted with an oath; the sudden imperative; an exclamation of comic impatience or spleen; all these give us a shining conviction of the intensely lived reality of a voice which seems to imply, at the moment of reading, less a persona than a person; less of a literary fabrication than an urgent speaking voice. 'For Godsake hold your tongue' drowns out the garrulity of an implied speaker, the drift of whose harangue we construct from the expostulations of the reply. The amused and marvelling reader tastes the pleasures proper to eavesdropping from the dramatic immediacy of the words-on-the-page. Each opening is a challenge to the imagination. It records the passionate assertiveness of an identity which demands to be heard *now*, imposing its claims, needs, arguments or boasts upon the reader's attention, with violent intensity or tender intimacy.

Strangely, the poems' difficulty does not detract from this illusion of vivid immediacy, though King James is said to have quipped that Donne's 'verses were like ye peace of God they passed all understanding' (*Heritage*, 74), and Ben Jonson to have predicted 'That Done himself for not being understood would perish' (*Heritage*, 70). Donne had been a student of law, theology, rhetoric, and philosophy, upon whose complex intellectual structures he elaborated mind-stretching images (the so-called Metaphysical conceits) in a wit whose subtlety and compressed grammatical expression are equalled only by its stunning tactical swerves and leaps into an illogic proper to the cunning sleights of the mind working at speed and under stress. The very vagaries and aberrations of this striving intelligence have a compulsive effect in begetting in a reader the sense that here, on the page, a living mind in the crises and turmoils of its life has succeeded in transferring a genuine, and somehow still-living, genetic or psychological imprint of an individual, heart and soul. In short, we feel we 'know' Donne.

That impression should not be discounted, for it records a response to a very real quality in the lyrics: an illusion of passionate and private confession which, though it has been buried between the covers of a book for over three centuries, carries a sense of the here-and-now. The Satires and Elegies make free with the obscene; the *Songs and Sonets* are frequently transgressive and heretical in their sexual attitudes and their reaction against the conventions of Elizabethan love-poetry and literary language itself. The Divine Poems are in a different way revolutionary. Donne's *avant-garde* modernity was perceived by contemporaries, who recognized in him an original, dispensing with 'servile imitation' and rejecting with contumely the smooth, melodious metrics of Tudor poetry, for 'to the awe of thy imperious wit | Our stubborne language bends'.[1] But this impression of modernity has lasted as long as the poems: Sarah Jewett, in a letter of 1889, reflected that she had been reading 'an old copy of Donne's poems with perfect delight. They seem new to me just now, even the things I knew best' (*Heritage*, 491). This is true to many readers' experience of Donne, the novelty of whose poems does not derive simply from those far-fetched conceits and odd quirks which affected Dr Johnson so equivocally ('Who but Donne would have thought that a good man is a telescope?') (*Heritage*, 223). In Donne, the scintillating quality of new discovery or suggestion resides in the very breathings, cadences, and idioms, and unanalysably outlasts many readings, as if the ink were only just dry on the page. During the early twentieth century, the poems achieved a new status of modernity through their rehabilitation in the canon by T. S. Eliot, in part as covert justification of his own writing practice: 'A thought to Donne was an experience; it modified his sensibility'.[2] That sense of the poetry's intellectual passion or passionate intelligence as occasioned by a vivid experience of the whole creative personality expresses not only Eliot's belief in the triumph of synthesis in Donne, but a familiar feeling that he knows, with a peculiar intimacy, is in touch with, the temperament that produced the poetry.

Some such personal impression is almost inescapable with Donne. So dynamic is his compulsion to beget his 'I' in or on us that we almost inevitably go away marked, kindled, or even rather bruised by the pressure of the identity on which he focuses. The poems are acts of attempted domination, using not only the imperative verb but every trick in the rhetorical book, to make his signature live in the reader. The love-poems force entry through passionate endearment, assertion of possession or sexual drive, lurid sexual fantasy, or sometimes a kind of thrilling calm which consummates the most hyperbolical poems:

> These burning fits but meteors bee,
>   Whose matter in thee is soone spent.
> Thy beauty,'and all parts, which are thee,
>   Are unchangeable firmament.
>
> Yet t'was of my minde, seising thee,
>   Though it in thee cannot persever.
> For I had rather owner bee
>   Of thee one houre, then all else ever.

('A Feaver', ll. 21–8)

Two ravishing gestures, memorable for their reckless rightness and the compression of their epigrammatic form, flare out against one another in heart-stopping contrast. The first is the 'unchangeable firmament', which fills the line and stops the stanza with its ponderingly, ponderously measured claim to her absolute perfection. The second is the more literally ravishing gesture of violently intense sexual possession ('seising thee'), timed to one mere hour in the midst of impermanence and glamorizing its sensual maleness ('owner . . . of thee') as heroic defiance of 'all else ever'. These poems possess us while we appropriate them, turning their splendours to our own use in the many moods of love. And simultaneously their authenticity as testaments of what seems to be lived experience plagues us with an itch to know or guess the biographical circumstances which generated them, so as to possess them more completely. This very human, though not necessarily aesthetically justified, yen is baffled in various instructive ways — instructive because they compel us to recognize that the very personal Donne by whom we are haunted may be in good part a familiar spirit of our own projection.

The present study cannot pretend to be free of such haunting, for, though I shall question the very foundations of the relationship between the life and the work, it is inevitable that much study of the full range of Donne's work will produce the uncanny likeness of a ghostly face in one's mind. I imagine this to myself as if it were a thin apparition constituted of a medium's ectoplasm: fabricated, of course, by my own imagination in the attempt to understand the diverse moods and languages of the poems, and using an abstemious handful of the facts that are known about Donne's life. Donne himself was insatiably curious about the possibility of his own survival after death. He opens his own grave and spies in at his amorous skeleton ('The Relique'); he maliciously promises to return from the dead and manifest himself to that 'fain'd vestall', his rejecting mistress: 'Then shall my ghost come to thy bed . . . ' ('The Apparition', l.4). In 1631, preparing for his own death, and having dispensed a number of lively and grisly sermons about the mortifying stink and slime to which we are finally reduced, he posed for his portrait wearing his shroud and standing upon an urn, so that an artist could sketch a design for a monument. This he kept at his bedside to study himself as a corpse-to-be. Such foresight is ambivalent, for it at once exposes and defends. The monument that commemorated his passing also solidified his ego for all time. It was inconceivable and intolerable that there should come a time when his ego should be extinguished. Hence, if our speculations about the relation of his life and work resemble a kind of séance in which we conjure delusions from the fragmentary testaments that betray and belie what they pretend to reveal, it is also true that Donne himself went a long way towards the soliciting of our project. His wit was a way of outwitting the crass logic of death: by imagining Donne undone, he verbally dominated his mortality, reconstituting himself as an eternal *revenant*. 'Can ghosts die?' he asked in 'The Computation' (l. 10).

He lived in pun, as a natural element. Two-faced, three-angled, and self-multiplying ambiguity of meaning was paradoxically the only place where he felt safe. Double meaning was his sanctuary or fastness. My own ghostly picture of Donne is of a face whose moods endlessly and restlessly change, rarely still or tranquil, but accomplishing from time to time the solace of an amazed repose. These changeable moods are themselves so unstable that they can imply their own opposite: they do not evolve but dissolve. Underlying them all is an emptiness for which he several times sought words, an impossible conjuring trick, given that such states of mind are by their very nature negative and wordless. In, for instance, 'A nocturnall upon S. Lucies Day', the sombre cadences reach to the depths of 'absence, darknesse, death; things which are not' (l. 18). In 1607–8 he wrote a treatise defending suicide, *Biathanatos*:

> I have often such a sickly inclination; and whether it be because I had my first breeding and conversation with men of a suppressed and afflicted religion, accustomed to the despite of death and hungry of an imagined martyrdom ... whensoever any affliction assails me, methinks I have the keys of the prison in mine own hand, and no remedy presents itself so soon to my heart as mine own sword.[3]

However, to write a treatise is not to be suicidal: the 'keys of the prison' in this instance were supplied by the pen with which he wrote his way out of danger. The manuscript *Biathanatos* bridged the abyss it described, just as the act of writing the words 'absence, darknesse, death' and 'nothing' fixed them as something; gave them and him a standing. Donne's self-consciousness is legendary. He observed himself in fascination; then watched himself looking at himself; imagined others observing him, and, whilst playing both to

5

mirror and gallery, built into the poetry adroit systems of irony and self-mockery which would make tone hard to gauge and meaning and direction semi-decipherable. Through such manipulations, the great exhibitionist acquired the paradoxical art of the vanishing act. Secrecy was a major theme of his self-declaration: 'to keepe that hid' ('The undertaking', ll. 4, 28) was a motto, and 'make no noise' ('A Valediction: forbidding mourning', l. 5) a message of his poetry. He curses, with pathological extravagance (laughing up his sleeve), 'Who ever guesses, thinks, or dreams he knowes | Who is my mistris' ('The Curse', ll. 1–2). Such public advertisement of private secrets naturally arouses a curiosity to taste the allure of forbidden fruit, which, openly available, might be found quite bland and prosaic. Hence, Donne's lyric voice both licenses our sense of familiarity by its intimacy of address and prohibits it by far-fetched guessing-games and the claim of an élite specialness.

Riddles demand to be solved. *'John Donne, Ann Donne, Un-done'*, he is said to have punned in a letter to his wife, during his disgrace of 1602, when, as the Lord Keeper, Sir Thomas Egerton's secretary and MP for Brackley, he revealed that he had secretly married his employer's 16-year-old niece, Ann More, daughter of the Lieutenant of the Tower of London. This offence against common and canon law was the most spectacular in a series of catastrophic miscalculations in a life singularly rich in *faux pas*. His capacity for offending patrons on whose benefactions he sought to depend was wonderful, as witness his over-familiarity with Lady Bedford in 1612 (see Bald, 275), and the gaffe in a sermon of 1627 in which his tactless reference to Queen Henrietta Maria angered Charles I and had to be apologized for. Donne's 'I' seems to have filled his own horizons, so as to block out the reality of other people's susceptibilities. His marriage to Ann More was a *faux pas* (in so far as it demolished his driving secular ambitions) which carries with it a potent glamour, accompanied by temptation to the reader of the love-poems to attach them to the ghost of a biographical context. This has often been done without much external or internal evidence beyond the aphrodisiac conviction that, because some poems seem so deeply felt, they must be addressed to his wife; whereas others should be attributed to relationships with equally solid earlier 'mistresses'. In fact we know little about the dating of the *Songs and Sonets* and nothing very detailed about the womanizing youth of Donne, beyond a very few contemporary comments ('a great visiter of Ladies'[4]), and his own later much-repeated regrets for the lewd sins of his youth. Some biographers become so retrospectively intimate with their subject's mind that they seem to claim a keyhole-peeping cognisance:

> The marriage of John and Ann Donne is on the evidence we have one of the most ideal and complete in the history of the institution; never was a couple more truly one flesh — that was an ideal Donne had always had, in his attitude to love, and it is revealed in the poems written both before and after his marriage. In *The Canonization*, he sees Ann and himself as one being, a Phoenix . . .[5]

A God's-eye-view of human matrimony here combines with the view of the fly on the bedroom wall to attest to an ideality which, if true, must have qualified as the eighth wonder of the world. The critic, Derek Parker, has canonized the marriage, infatuated, on the one hand, by the glamour of Donne's all-for-love gesture and spellbound on the other, by the giant inflations and hyperboles of the poems. ('All here in one bed lay ... Princes doe but play us' ... 'You whom reverend love I Made one anothers hermitage ... Who did the whole worlds soule contract ... ' ('The Canonization', ll. 37–8, 40). The profoundly moving cadences of the love-poems can seem to a reader as sacramental and conclusive as wedding-rings, gifts offered to one woman, for life. Both 'The Sunne Rising' and 'The Canonization' imply (through satiric allusion to a king rather than a queen, suggestions of exclusion from the social mainstream, and the allusion in 'The Canonization' to the 'plaguie Bill', probably the Plague of 1603–4) a composition-date within the reign of James I. The critic therefore takes their confessionalism at face value, assuming that the thumbnail sketches of social climbers scrambling for office in a world from which the lovers are excluded must refer directly to Donne's world-forfeiting marriage:

> Take you a course, get you a place,
> Observe his honour, or his grace,
> Or the Kings reall, or his stamped face
> Contemplate, what you will, approve,
> So you will let me love.

> (ll. 5–9)

The key-word 'love', ending the first and last lines of each stanza, provides a guiding rhyme which recurs twenty times in forty-five lines, and rounds out the area of the lover's profession as an élite alternative space. The persona claims and consecrates his private marginality as a new centre, his shared exclusion as a rare exclusiveness from the place-seeking sycophancy of court, ecclesiastical palace, or mercantile exchange. So superb is the gesture, with its fling of exasperated temper ('For Godsake hold your tongue ...' l. 1), and so strange and moving its oscillation between mockery, self-mockery, cockiness, awe, religion, and deep tenderness ('one another's hermitage' (l. 38)), that it is indeed difficult to resist the temptation to read the poem as a personal testament to the poet's marriage and its aftermath, along with a companion piece like 'The Sunne Rising', and 'A Valediction: forbidding mourning', which Donne's friend and biographer, Izaak Walton, said (but not until the fourth edition of his *Life*) had been written for his wife when he left her in 1611 to go abroad with the Drurys.

How far should we resist such biographical temptations? Superficially, they do little harm, reinforcing the reader's power to respond to the emotion conjured by the poetry. But they will be specious visits to Cloudcuckooland if based on patent fallacies. Thus Helen Gardner argues for resistance to Walton's attribution on grounds (in themselves rather quaint) that, in the 'Valediction', Donne's injunction to secrecy 'is not an argument to use to a wife, who has no need to hide her grief at her husband's absence'.[6] Her insistence that the 'Valediction' must therefore have a mistress in mind is based on the same literality as breathes the ghost of Ann Donne into the centre of the love-poems. But Donne himself wrote to a friend that 'I did best when I had least truth for my subjects'.[7] Donne's letters bear witness to an aghast quality in his experience of the aftermath of marriage which should reinforce our sense of the obliquity in which poetry stands to life. Poverty, dependency, boredom, illness, and claustrophobia in the company of a growing family of children bred melancholy and aggravation: the dreariness of the humdrum which nowhere finds a place in Donne's imaginative world. In fact one assumes that the creative world insists upon its exclusion. The letters represent Donne's keeping constant company with his wife as a duty of allegiance, having transplanted her from her privileged background to the grind of squalid circumstances and incessant child-bearing. 'I stand like a tree which once a year beares, though no fruit, this mast of children' (*Letters*, i. 154): this is confessional where the poems are not. The image is pregnant with ironies. It represents his loneliness, estrangement, and rootfast inertia. As the tree of genealogy, it stands for the relentless incontinence of biology; as a parody tree of knowledge, it expresses the absence of intellectual stimulation. This 'mast of children' — a litter of beechmast or acorns — reveals his stupefaction and repressed irritation in the midst of a cacophonous family. Most profoundly, the tree-image feminizes him. That subjection to fruitless procreation to which nature and culture combined to condemn women is now the progenitor's lot. Apart from travels in Europe with Sir Walter Chute in 1605–6 and with the Drurys in 1611–12, and intermittent visits to patrons and friends, the years from 1602 until his ordination in 1615 were spent confined to domesticity, mainly in a cramped, draughty house in Mitcham. Part of the gall of these years derives from the fact that the thrust of his worldly male ambitions had landed him in a woman's world. Hence the temptation to read the love-poems as literal personal documents comes with thorns and briars attached.

The present study takes the large general patterns and sweep of Donne's individual life as a way of guessing out hints and clues to configurations of meaning in his poetry, so as to avoid impaling itself on those thorns. More important will be the cultural, historical, and religious forces (often stormily contradictory) which cross-biased to shape Donne and to which he was constrained to form a vivid complex of attitudes and responses. The sense of a living intelligence which leaps off the page to stir our own minds was a product of Catholic and Protestant antagonism which met in him — born of a devoutly Roman Catholic family in a Protestant country — and fought out in the battleground of his psyche an equivalent of the religious wars of Europe. In that struggle, issuing ultimately in his ordination and elevation to the Deanery of St Paul's, issues of social class cross-bias with problems of religious and political allegiance. To be born in 1572, the ambitious son of a successful London ironmonger, set him scaling the rungs of a social ladder from which affiliation to a banned religion would disqualify him. In Elizabethan England, harbouring a Catholic priest and hearing mass were criminal offences; professing Catholics could not receive university degrees and were debarred from holding civic or political office. It was possible to keep your head low and avoid trouble. But Donne's family was proudly conspicuous in its recusancy. On his mother's side, he was related to Sir Thomas More, the Catholic 'martyr'. His great-uncle, Thomas Heywood, a former monk, was executed for saying mass; two uncles, Ellis and

Jasper Heywood, became Jesuits; Donne's mother was profoundly devout, and his brother Henry died in Newgate in 1593, having been arrested for harbouring a Roman Catholic priest in his chambers at Lincoln's Inn. Donne's life is one long, rueful abdication from this allegiance. All his life-events, including his marriage, should be seen shadowed by his Catholic origins, from the early date of his Oxford and Cambridge education (avoiding taking the degree) to his volunteering for military service in the Essex expeditions to Cadiz in 1596 and the Azores in 1597, thereby gaining credentials as a true Elizabethan patriot. He detached himself from his Roman origins with guilt and pain, under the impulse of a power-hungry drive. The prose-works, *Pseudo-Martyr* (1610) and *Ignatius His Conclave* (1611), were a favour-currying attempt to endorse the Oath of Allegiance to James I and an attack on the Jesuits. Remorseful terror of apostasy shadowed his progress and tainted his spiritual well-being, even when, as an ordained Church of England priest, he had sealed his choice irreversibly. Scrupulous study of the differences between the Reformed and Roman Churches in which Walton says he was already engaged at about the age of 20 when he 'begun seriously to survey, and consider the Body of Divinity' (Bald, 68) could co-exist with crafty desires slipping along the broad route to advancement.

In the mature Donne, not only Catholic and Protestant but Jesuitical and Calvinist, truth-seeker and self-seeker, incompatibly exist. If we are all pages on to which history inscribes itself, his page was dynamic in its complexities. Through Donne, the Counter-Reformation (with its Baroque and Mannerist intensities and obliquities and its Ignatian devotional exercises) shines on to a page illuminated also by the darkness and radiances of Calvinist introspection. Like light through new-made windows, the discoveries of what Donne and his contemporaries called the Copernican 'new Philosophy' cast a disturbing gloss on the same mental page, displacing earth and humanity as the centre of the God-made universe, while the telescope of Galileo magnified and contracted the field of vision in the blink of an eye. The word on that page was equally disturbed, as early linguistic theories (exemplified by Bacon and Montaigne) queried language's ambiguity, its indifference to and evasion of truth in the wake of humanism: 'Words, words, words' (*Hamlet*, III. ii. 192). The page upon which history and culture shone their contending lamps rested on the unstable surface of a political world in crisis, drifting towards absolutism and the fracture of the nation that would culminate in the Civil Wars of 1642. Donne did not live to see this dénouement, dying in 1631, but the dynamics of the religious, political, and theological perplexity into which he was born must be viewed as shaping if not dictatorial elements in the creation of his poetry.

If he was a born performer, he acted therefore in a theatre of doubt, spreading far beyond his immediate environment on a continental and ultimately global scale — since this was an era of colonialist imperialism, whose adventures and ethics are written into his poetry of sexual and spiritual discovery. While Donne was a thinking mind, vividly alert to the implications of intellectual change and controversy, he was also a receptor, being thought through by the divided mind of the period. *Hamlet* casts doubt on the scripting of the parts played by actors on the world's stage, together with the status of the language assigned or fabricated. A Montaignian scepticism could seem the only credible reaction to the flux of definition created by these convulsions in the European mind. Our hunt for Donne's 'real' self is likely to prove as incapable of satisfaction as Rosencrantz's and Guildenstern's for Hamlet's if we ignore or deny the fact that for Donne the 'self' was in doubt. The more he looked at or for it, the more it vanished. Existing as a process in time and subject to contingency and interpretation, it was possible to say 'that now I We are not just those persons, which we were ...' ('Womans constancy', ll. 4–5); 'You are both fluid, chang'd since yesterday' ('The second Anniversarie', l. 393). The river keeps its name and course, but moment by moment new waters displace the old. 'Our selves', he wrote, are 'what we know not' (Carey, 170). Donne's scepticism has much in common with Montaigne's, who, in 'On Experience' quoted the same image of water-displacement as the condition of human life and knowledge. Montaigne praised the dissatisfactions of intellectual endeavour, whose 'food is wonder, search and ambiguity ... an irregular and perpetual motion, without model and without goal'. He denied the integrity of biography, for: 'Not only do I find it difficult to connect our actions one with another, but I have trouble too in designating each one separately by some principal quality, so ambiguous and variegated do they appear in different lights.'[8] But Montaigne's amiable tolerance of doubt and foible stands in contrast to Donne's violently complex reaction, which writes doubt into his texts through their very structure: eccentric and skewed vision, errant logic, tonal shifts, extremism verging on self-parody, insecure but categorical self-assertion.

God was beyond doubt; literally, beyond it. This is where Donne parts company with modernist alienation, whose query about the self attaches to a cosmic sense of ontological uncertainty. When Donne famously announced that 'new Philosophy calls all in doubt' ('The first Anniversary', l. 205), he meant 'all except the Almighty' who is beyond the 'all' of the universe: too far beyond, perhaps, for comfort. If Donne seems never to have doubted God's existence, he was however seldom sure of God's relation to his own unstable self. He called the atheist 'Poore intricated soule! Riddling, perplexed, labyrinthicall soule!' (*Sermons*, vi. 72) but these adjectives might mirror with equal justice the maze of corridors in his own breast. To the opacity of the shape-shifting self was added the fear (in essence sexual) of damaging or losing it altogether. Human trust — more especially in a woman, for his male friendships blossomed — was difficult, since it involved exposure and yielding of the evasive heart and tenderer ego. Loss of face, which was nearly as troubling — especially in the 'Mitcham' period, when he was desperately in need of patronage and cash — could be adapted to a commanding posture of literary self-abasement, so extreme in its hyperbolical inflation of the dedicatee that it verges on parody. Lady Bedford and Magdalen Herbert are blasphemously flattered in the Verse Letters by gross magnifications of traditional Petrarchan compliment. His wicked pen informed Lady Bedford that by Reason and Faith, 'wee reach divinity, that's you' ('To the Countesse of Bedford', l. 2), the pert 'that's you' carrying a silent inflection to the effect that she who could believe such stuff would believe anything. His praise co-exists with a swashbuckling misogyny. Sycophancy to the Countess of Huntingdon is preluded with offensive witticisms about Eve's and woman's defectiveness disqualifying them from state or ecclesiastical office ('To the Countesse of Huntingdon', ll. 3–4). Virtue, fallen in the general entropy, has 'fled to heaven, that's heavenly things, that's you' (l. 22), the same slightly gormless trick that he had offered to Lady Bedford, supplemented with additional thought on rarefications of purity, each of which seems brazenly bidding for cash on delivery. 'I hate extreams', wrote the extremist, preposterously, in 'The Autumnall', his praise of the 32-year old Mrs Herbert, who may or may not have relished comparison of her middle-aged wrinkles to trenches in which Love sits like an anchorite (ll. 45, 15–16). Hence the riddling, perplexed, labyrinthical wit which elsewhere magnifies his image as a lover here serves up a fantastic tribute which derides its object by reconstructing her as an ingenious artefact of his own design. His arrogant dependency sought to stimulate in these aristo-cratic women an answering and remunerative dependency, by transmuting the base art of eulogy into a daring act of pride. It did not work very well. It has been well said of Donne that 'his brain went to his head' (Simmel Goldberg), blocking out the obvious. Wryly, he was capable of seeing that too.

If the self was in doubt, so were its projection and inscription. Donne's fascination with his own name has a compulsive quality. Because our names are 'givens', imposed by genealogy and antecedent to self-consciousness, they have at once a natural-seeming familiarity ('I am Donne') and an artificial foreignness ('I am called Donne'). Fortuitously, the poet's surname was a pun carrying a variety of implications, flowing from the verb *to do*. An active doer, worldly, careerist, urban, and sexually and socially thrusting, he might welcome his name as a not unflattering mirror, but, burdened with the passivity of its past-participle status, would also reflect that to be *done* meant to be finished, or done for, and that the addition of a negative prefix left him *undone* (with its possible sexual connotations). In what he thought of as a death-bed poem, he played with the slipperiness of the self he longed to cede to God: 'When thou hast done, thou hast not done' ('Hymne to God the Father', ll. 5, 11). Only when he could push the name into alignment with the rhyme 'sonne' (the atoning Son of God) could he resolve the conundrum, for God's self, unlike his own, stood stable and firm for all eternity. When he asked God to 'sweare by thy self' (l. 15) to be with him in mercy at death, he desired God to take the oath 'by God', invoking the only name which had perfect spiritual and therefore linguistic congruity with its referent. God's name and self affirmed and confirmed the bond between the poet's own shifty name and eloquent self, so that, 'having done that, Thou hast done, I I feare no more' (ll. 17–18). When God has closed with Donne, the poem achieves closure.

In an earlier poem, 'A Valediction: of my name, in the window', Donne reflects on the curious detachability of a signature from the self it represents. He engraves his name with a diamond on the pane of his mistress's window, an act of self-projection in a text on a transparent medium which mimes the equivocation latent in the art of writing, and the distance between the name and the self. Almost immediately, both the meaning and the medium are brought into question, for, while the window has qualities which contradict its transparency, so the 'I' of the poem's claim to be 'all confessing, and through-shine' reveals itself as an optical illusion:

> 'Tis much that Glasse should bee
> As all confessing, and through-shine as I,
> 'Tis more, that it shewes thee to thee,
> And cleare reflects thee to thine eye.
> But all such rules, loves magique can undoe,
> Here you see mee, and I am you.

(ll. 7–12)

The 'I' of the stanza announces itself as a text. The medium upon which the text has been engraved is ambivalent, for, though 'Tis much' that the glass is transparent, 'Tis more' that it constitutes a reflective surface, throwing back the image of the beholder upon her own scrutiny. However, since the medium has been tampered with (by the inscription of the name), so the relationship of 'I' as the inscriber and 'I' as the eyewitness is guilefully destabilized under pressure of Donne's excitable narcissism. Exploiting the pun on his own name by the tricky magic of spell-binding assertion, Donne 'undoes' the woman's autonomous identity (l. 11). The window of the poem throws back her own mirror-image labelled with the name of Donne, and the stanza completes itself with the triumphant sophistry that 'I am you'. *Trompe l'œil* illusionism becomes not just the method but the subject of the poem: textual representation, covering for the absence of the lover, becomes a playful bid for sexual possession.

But not only does the name exist in distinction from the person it designates: it floats, as the poem develops, into ever greater estrangement. And, in its exile, it troubles the relationship between the reader and the text of the poem. 'Here you see mee, and I am you', taunts not only the fictional girl but the reader who, in the act of reading, is addressed as 'you' but who also identifies herself or himself with and as 'I'. We oscillate between the parties in the dialogue, between nominative and accusative, first and second persons, speaker and addressee. And the poem's dashing,

14

provocative intelligence ingeniously stirs us to think about this relationship. The poem reflects upon its own textual processes and stratagems. Although the 'Valediction' claims in Stanza III to maintain the fixity and fidelity of the textual identity of the speaker against erosion by 'showers and tempests' (ll. 15), the speaker is nervously aware that the name, abandoned in his absence, has been consigned to the problematic area of open interpretation or, worse, to the possibility that it will be simply ignored. To catch her eye he loads the name with the glittering wit of a *tour de force* of novel significations, retrieving it from anonymity, as a *memento mori amoris* and then promising the return of the body of which it is a skeletal mnemonic: 'Or thinke this ragged bony name to bee I My ruinous Anatomie' (ll. 23–4). The microscopically realistic and the surreal combine in this sharply visual image. How can a name be ragged and bony? As an awkward system of irregular scratches on the pane, his signature records the bare bones of his identity, the 'rafters' (l. 28) of the house of his body waiting to be fleshed out on his return. Donne's comic gift seems to mock the extravaganza of his own fantasy-life, even as his fantasy solicits admiration and an underlying turbulence stirs the surface brilliance of the wit. Later, 'my trembling name' (l. 44) quivers as his mistress throws open the window in response to a new suitor. He turns the name into a talismanic fetish interrupting her communication with a rival by appropriating his signature in a letter and unconsciously persuading her to address her reply to himself (Stanzas IX and X).

In the course of the poem, the representation has shown its capacity to detach itself more and more fully from the representor, who is, however, fascinated by its promiscuity and seeks to control it to his own ends through reckless acts of commandeering and exhibitionistic wit. In the end, he acknowledges, it was all 'idle talke' (l. 65). Smitten by the loose and problematic relationship between symbol and thing symbolized, between mind and action, narrative and life, writer and reader, text and identity, language and meaning, he grounds an exploratory art in the ambivalent medium of a self-referring language which he seeks, in poem after poem, to dominate. Scepticism and irony constantly undercut, with caustic intelligence, this claim to potency, with the awareness that, while we play games with language, language plays games with us. Something in the arbitrary nature of language (Bacon's 'words absolutely force the understanding, put all things in confusion')[9] and something in the devious nature of the human mind (Montaigne's 'the mind ... is all the time turning, contriving, and entangling itself in its own work, like a silk-worm')[10], combined to defeat Donne's project. One of the spectacular glories of his achievement is that his poems have the brains to investigate, through irony, self-consciousness, and sophisticated philosophical focus, the processes and conditions of their defeat. If, in 'A Valediction: of my name, in the window', Donne seems to be conjuring with the optical magic of a perspective-glass, those fashionable toys of the period, multiplying images and angles to bend light and skew vision, he is also watching his own consciousness in the act of manipulating perception, registering the psyche's stresses and sublimations. Even when, as the Dean of St Paul's, he had achieved not only a position of eminence but also a thunderous oratorical success as the giver of the hair-raising, spine-chilling sermons with which he wooed, dominated, and menaced his congregation, he retained this sceptical relativism. For the path to the pulpit was also the road to Calvary; he had to shear the last vestiges of the bond to his Roman Catholic father in order to make this ascent. Hence his vehement but anxious ecumenism which sought to see 'a *Rome*, or a *Wittemberg*, or a *Geneva*' (Catholic, Lutheran, or Calvinist) as 'all virtuall beams of one Sun' (*Letters*, 29) and asked in Holy Sonnet XVIII, 'Show me deare Christ, thy spouse', representing the Spirit — grotesquely — as a holy harlot, of promiscuous invitation (ll. 11–14). The convulsive conflicts of these sonnets and some of the sermons imply the extraordinary double perspective of one who is able to bear witness with eagle-eyed detachment to a process which only its textualization saves from becoming a nervous breakdown. As Dean and royal chaplain, Donne rose in a sudden meteoric burst from the 'nothing' he had called himself in the 'Mitcham' years to a heady elevation. In his own mind he was a king, or more than a king, for 'His Ministers are an Earth-quake, and shake an earthly soul' (*Sermons*, vii. 396). Whereas in the love-poetry he had claimed royal standing in and over his mistress's body, now he could king it over the King himself, preaching frequently at court. His last sermon, given before King Charles I and entitled 'Deaths Duell', was 'called by his Majesties household The Doctor's own funerall Sermon' (Bold, 486). The cadaverous, dying man was his own text. Hamlet had taken Holy Orders.

Donne's poetry resembles a voyage of discovery. His inflations mime the magnifications of the newly discovered telescope. But the discoveries also demonstrate the problematic nature of what is explored and conquered through vision. The revelatory lens amplifies the field of inconstancy. 'O my America! my new-found-land', exclaims the colonizing lover of Elegy XIX ('Going to Bed' ll. 28, 30), 'How blest am I in this discovering thee!', where 'discover' puns on 'dis-cover', stripping bare; 'Let sea-discoverers to new worlds have gone', the lover in 'The good-morrow' allows (l. 12). If Donne imports the Elizabethan imperialist lust of conquest into his poetry, transferring it to the zone of a phallic expansionism, the excited optimism of this privateering dash for new worlds does not go unqualified. The discovery of new continents on earth and planetary bodies in the heavens played on a mind easily made insecure and quick to intellectualize his insecurities, for it suggested that the earth under our feet was neither safe nor stable. The Copernican earth took off and whirled round the sun, planetary orbits defected and extended from circles to ellipses, to be joined by the new 'stars' discovered by Galileo's telescope (actually the moons of Jupiter and Saturn). Donne in his European journeys may well have picked up one of the cheap telescopes which, within a year of Galileo's *Star-Messenger* (1610), were selling in Venice for a couple of scudi each. *Ignatius His Conclave*, with its image of moon-travel, implies that he had read Kepler's *Dream*, in which the astronomer is viewed as a cosmonaut: at any rate, Kepler himself thought Donne had read it. But Donne's apprehension of global and cosmic discovery is tense with dismayed consciousness that its novelty threatens and unsettles. The new light gained by science revealed a world darker than previously conceived The 'new Philosophy arrests the Sunne, I And bids the passive earth about it runne' he complained in a verse epistle ('To the Countesse of Bedford', ll. 37–8). Peripheral and passive, its ego insulted, the earth (with its cargo of vicious, degenerate man) forfeits its self-gratifying delusion of centrality and is subjected to laws which demoralizingly bind ('arrest') the sun by immobilizing it. The effect of Donne's emotive description is to suggest loss of volition and security. Later, a sermon comments on the unhinging effect of Copernicanism's denial of 'settlednesse' to the earth — not, he emphasizes, that this was news to him (*Sermons*, vii. 234). The restless earth is a fit home for the fluctuating self.

A justly celebrated passage in 'The first Anniversary' (1611) wittily condenses this sense of disturbance and disintegration:

And new Philosophy calls all in doubt,
The Element of fire is quite put out;
The Sun is lost, and th'earth, and no mans wit
Can well direct him where to looke for it.
And freely men confesse that this world's spent,
When in the Planets, and the Firmament
They seeke so many new; they see that this
Is crumbled out againe to his Atomies.
'Tis all in peeces, all cohaerence gone;
All just supply, and all Relation:
Prince, Subject, Father, Sonne, are things forgot,
For every man alone thinkes he hath got
To be a Phoenix, and that there can bee
None of that kinde, of which he is, but hee.

(ll. 205–18)

The passage occurs in the first of two hyper-inflated elegies for a young woman, Elizabeth Drury, the blasphemous excesses of which Jonson reported Donne as justifying as descriptions of 'the Idea of a Woman and not as she was' (*Heritage*, 69). The death of this 'Idea' is viewed as the world's catastrophe: soul-forsaken, it is left in the condition of a mortifying ball of decaying matter. The poet–pathologist produces the report of his inquest on 'the worlds carcasse' ('The first Anniversary', l. 439). The 'new Philosophy' passage supplies the pathologist's credentials, the compelling Copernican analysis being shown as agent of loss of focus in the whole intellectual community. Where only doubt is certain, the problem becomes, literally, *where to look*, and the drift is towards multiplicity of eyeline and opinion, pursuit of novel perception, and a painful reversal of the Lucretian atomic theory, so that all motion tends towards disintegration. The pieties of civil and family relationship also submit to this entropic process, as in *King Lear*, with its comparable breakdown of natural law. But the passage also has a startling modernity for a twentieth-century reader, an equivalent of the apocalyptic vision of cultural upheaval in Yeats's 'Things fall apart; the centre cannot hold' (*The Second Coming*, l.3).

On the face of it, the vision is depressive. To have 'lost' the sun is to perish for want of vital warmth; to have 'lost' the earth is to be a refugee, bereaved of vital bearings. But the effect is by no means depressive. Donne's couplet art displays an aphoristic brilliance that congratulates itself as it proceeds, on its contraction of universal chaos into the order and discipline of rhyming couplets. Jaunty rhymes ('no man's wit I ... looke for it') and the suggestion of colloquial extemporaneousness ('this world's spent'), along with satiric contempt ('thinkes he hath got I To be a Phoenix'), combine to counteract the threat of disorder, at least to the persona, who has the measure of it. But the anti-depressive quality goes deeper than this. Exultation has never been foreign to apocalyptic prophecy. Jeremiah's 'O earth, earth, earth, hear the word of the LORD' (Jer. 22: 29) and St John of Patmos 'For the day of his wrath is come ...' (Rev. 6: 17) speak with zest and vigour of impending calamity: the very act of articulation exempts and immunizes the speaker from prostration before the condition which it belongs to him to define. On another level, there was a sense in which Donne was uniquely at home in the sphere of 'doubt', which signified simultaneous threat and thrill. To be 'lost' is to be free of what one might call 'parental' constraints, wandering Oedipally away from the given co-ordinates, to trespass like a wandering star to the limits of a universe which, because all in it tends towards the absurd, permissively licenses absurdity. Where nothing is demonstrable as finally true, there is also scanty possibility of provable error.

The emotional complexity of this 'new' position of scepticism may be divined from a reading of Satire III, in which a highly charged, violently indignant voice denounces the religious errors of his time, which it enumerates and scourges one by one. The tongue of the speaker is a frenzied whiplash doling out correction in literally all directions. Taking his antagonist, an indeterminate, worldly 'thou', metaphorically by the throat ('O if thou dar'st, feare this ... O desperate coward, wilt thou seem bold ...' (ll. 15, 29)), he lambasts him with rhetorical questions — nine in the first thirty-two lines — to induce him to leave off his cocky posturings in favour of a more courageous holy fear of repercussions in the life to come. Then, from line 43, he savages the varieties of religious error current in his generation, from Catholicism, Calvinism, and Anglicanism to scepticism and ecumenism. 'Seeke true religion,' the satirist instructs. But where? No choice seems uncontaminated. All churches are chosen on perverse or unworthy grounds — for instance, Rome on the grounds that Truth was there a thousand years ago. The sceptical author of the poem rules out scepticism itself as a legitimate reaction to the life-and-death issues of religious commitment. To complicate the argument and emotion yet further, Donne twice invokes paternal authority. 'Thy' father's spirit looks down from heaven and sees his son, having betrayed his religious upbringing, damned (ll. 11–15); later the antagonist is instructed to 'ask thy father which is shee, I Let him aske his' (ll. 71–2). This fallback position on the authority of patriarchal tradition makes no kind of sense within a poem which disclaims merely human dictates in favour of painstaking inner search on the part of the questioning individual, who must carry the full burden of responsibility for his choice. In the face of this inconsistency, the logic of the poem disintegrates. I have queried the relationship of life to art, but there the poem's contradictions are illuminated (*not* resolved) by tentative application of the equivalent contradictions of the life. For who is 'thou' and who are the father and grandfather so strikingly invoked?

The argument upon which Donne's poems are founded is often so compelling, cunning, and stressful because it is waged against himself. Uneasy transactions with his own irresoluble contradictions are a root of the texts' psychological energy and twisty, self-duplicitous logic — like a pair of hands working at cross-purposes or a pair of eyes seeing double. If 'I' and 'thou' are both read as Donne, some of the manic quality of this poem, together with the dead-ends it offers, comes into focus. 'I' neglects to state that the father of 'thou' was a Roman Catholic, dead before the poet was 4 years old and assumed by the poem to be in Heaven. In the literal as opposed to the literary world, if Donne asks his father's blessing on the present tirade, his father must inevitably refuse it. For the questions which inspire the Satire break faith with his family; and yet, to renounce those questions is to break faith with his own life's ambitions and autonomy, together with the possibility of a new integrity, harrowingly and strenuously won. As late as the crises that precipitated the Holy Sonnets (mostly written around 1607–10), Donne was fantasizing his father looking down from his beatitude to judge his son's spiritual quest: how could his apostasy be read as 'white truth' (Holy Sonnet VIII, l. 8)? The self-condemning apostate has three options: to return to the True Church, which he cannot and will not do; to live in the body and the moment, like 'thou' of the early passages; or to take the arduous and solitary path of the interrogative soul through a landscape composed all of questionings, not only through uncertainties but also through indirections and circuitous mental processes. This pilgrimage is symbolized in the famous Hill of

Truth icon which dominates the Satire not only through its spectacular scale and ingenuity, but through the rugged mimesis by which Donne's metrics refuse the primrose path, miming the conflict between the hill's forbidding steepness and the determination of the climber's hard-breathing struggle for footholds and eventual ascent:

> Be busie to seeke her, beleeve mee this,
> Hee's not of none, nor worst, that seekes the best.
> To adore, or scorne an image, or protest,
> May all be bad; doubt wisely; in strange way
> To stand inquiring right, is not to stray;
> To sleepe, or runne wrong, is. On a huge hill,
> Cragged, and steep, Truth stands, and hee that will
> Reach her, about must, and about must goe;
> And what the hills suddennes resists, winne so;
> Yet strive so, that before age, deaths twilight,
> Thy Soule rest, for none can worke in that night.
> To will, implyes delay, therefore now doe:
> Hard deeds, the bodies paines; hard knowledge too
> The mindes indeavours reach, and mysteries
> Are like the Sunne, dazling, yet plaine to all eyes.
> Keepe the truth which thou hast found ...

> (ll. 74–89)

The unparalleled sublimity of this awesome vision derives from magnificence of imagery combined with raw power of articulation: the reader stands dwarfed. The dramatic hill which so disempowers us with the conviction of the puniness of our capacities is created by sublime fiat of Donne's overbearing intelligence. He places it suddenly before us, as a threat and a challenge. But if it is lofty, the narrative consciousness is loftier. The imperious voice which tells us that we know nothing and must scramble and strain for light is paradoxically omniscient on that topic. The poetry is never as confident as here, where it issues instructions on the route-map to be followed, in command after command, grounded in the authority of self-coined aphorism (ll. 75, 76–7, 77–8, 79, 84, 87–8, 89–90), elevated upon the dictatorial power of stressed imperative verbs ('doubt wisely ... now doe ... Keepe the truth') and commanding reiterations ('about must, and about must goe ... winne so ... Yet strive so ... hard deeds ... hard knowledge too'). The double 'must' achieves an initial status of apparent independence from its auxiliary function, by ellipsis, as if there were an urgent verb *to must*. All confirms the speaker's credentials as one who knows this journey well and has acquired the qualifications to issue this summons as a result of the throes of his own arduous ascent towards a personal truth. The hectoring voice is majestic in its certainties, a punchy speaking-voice impatient of (though assenting to) metrical control.

And yet, just as its subject is momentous labour through indirection, so also its message is calculatingly oblique. An apocalyptic tone, impelled by violently spontaneous rhythms, hurries the reader from rock to rock of the track of his argument: below, it seems, precipitous cliffs fall away and, as he urges us on, the declivities beneath are equalled by the lack of time allowed to accomplish the near-impossible task before nightfall. The headlong voice is at once authoritative and exciting: perhaps too much so, for its loyalties are split. The passage has a Protestant emphasis on the sacred importance of the personal pilgrimage, governed by the inner light of God's Grace: what Milton, who also dwelt on the multiplicity of Truth, was to call the path of the 'true wayfaring Christian'.[11] On the other hand, its emphasis on active labour ('none can worke in that night ... hard knowledge ... the minds indeavours') implies the Catholic doctrine of works. Open receptivity to the Divine Light is not emphasized but rather the programme of ratiocination and study by which Donne accomplished his own shift from Catholic to Anglican. In Holy Sonnet XIV he would comment on the corruption of human Reason, God's viceroy which is 'captiv'd' (to Satan) 'and proves weake or untrue'. He knew the mendacity of thought, its subservience to the self-satisfying ego. Leaning on that corrupted instrument, one goes wrong automatically, and all straight-line routes are aberrations; hence he champions the seeker who is willing to entrust himself to the devious or deviant path ('about must, and about must goe'). The passage identifies with extraordinary resonance a method of knowing and an integrity of stance in a fragmented, complex, and recognizably modern world. It defends the singular vision, whatever that may be, against the usurpation of political authorities over individual consciences, whether Catholic or Protestant: 'Foole and wretch', he thunders, 'wilt thou let thy Soule be tyed I To mans lawes ...?' (ll. 93–4). In the shadow of the Last Judgement, a late flurry of rhetorical questions flays the conformists who appeal to the authority of a Pope or a Luther (ll. 95–9).

But who is this 'foole and wretch'? The insult is thrust out from the page at our eyes as we (fools and wretches) read. But our act of reading subverts the intended trajectory of the rebuke. It ricochets back as *we* identify our own 'I' with the poem's 'I', to redirect 'foole and wretch' elsewhere. The poem's retort back against the writer as it hits the reader is a rebound which reflects the dynamic tension within the text itself, recording a fracture within the persona's consciousness between polarized aspects of himself. For the deepest conviction recounted by the poem is of psychic turbulence and dismay: the persona no more knows where to go or how to get there than we do. Hence the allegory, with stunning intensity, persuades us of the all-but-impossible character of the harrowing researches we *must* pursue; the absence of all compass-bearings except hope as we round the bend of the mountain in the direction of God-knows-what, on a path that runs in circles. Donne's mountain of Truth bears disturbing resemblance to the traditional Catholic symbol of the mountain of Purgatory, in whose lee Dante stood aghast: 'So high the summit, it outsoared the sight'.[12] Donne's pilgrimage, fraught with stress and effort, seems alike penitential. Purgatory, a concept jettisoned with his renunciation of Catholicism, seems transferred from the afterlife into the time-zone in which any progress must be made now, traverse and athwart the forbidding contour of the mountain, in the brief remaining span. The sense of crisis, of living in the moment of emergency, is a mood of Donne's highly wrought poetry throughout his life.

If we should read Donne in terms of his religious conflicts, so also his work is illuminated by being placed within the Baroque and Mannerist tradition in art and architecture. As a continentally travelled ex-Catholic, he had seen and internalized the principles that informed the Baroque perspectivism and relativistic distortions of spatial relationships in the cathedrals, monuments, and pictures of Counter-Reformation Europe. The towering sublimities of Mannerism, with its sensational tricks of the eye, intense chiaroscuro effects, and conscious violation of classical laws of humanist proportion, were related to a Catholic devotionalism on the one hand and the Copernican revolution on the other. Bernini's and Gaulli's forcing of dimensions and eyeline out of true so as to create a singular angle of vision delivers visual shocks that can operate like a blast into the head of the observer. A dome or ceiling breaches inner space and soars into the dynamic universe beyond.

23

Donne's exploding hypotaxes; his bending or inversion of spatial relationships ('one little room, an every where' ('The good-morrow', l. 11)), the cosmological pretensions of his love and the dazzling but troubled coruscations of his wit and imagery, come close to Mannerism. In El Greco, passionate dilations of space that curves and twists in obedience to the ardour of an imperious inner vision deny the primacy of considerations of statuesque and harmonious beauty. Violent foreshortenings, emphasis on the marginal or the spectator, and the dialectical tension of spiritual conflict are released into a dynamic grammar of paint. Mannerism's insistence that reality is not as we normally see it; its commitment to aberration and the pulling of the viewer's lazy eye along vistas of extension; its relentless invitation to us to admire and be amazed, are reflected in Donne's literary pyrotechnics. Both manner and matter is *trompe l'œil*. In 'The Canonization' future generations are made to invoke the dead lovers:

> And thus invoke us; You whom reverend love
>   Made one anothers hermitage;
> You, to whom love was peace, that now is rage;
>   Who did the whole worlds soule contract, and drove
>   Into the glasses of your eyes
>   So made such mirrors, and such spies,
> That they did all to you epitomize,
>   Countries, Townes, Courts: Beg from above
>   A patterne of your love!

(ll. 37–45)

The gigantic inflation of 'whole worlds soule' by pure force of linguistic fiat is condensed to the centimetre diameter of the omnivorous lovers' lens. Violent force (the emphatically placed verb 'drove') suggesting either a wounding or a powerful sexual penetration performs this diminution and internalization of the dimensions of external reality, and hence achieves imaginative appropriation of and dominance over it. This fantasy is played out with breath-taking élan, a Baroque sequence of *trompe l'œil* transformations in which world enters eye; eye becomes mirror; the posthumous lovers become spies through their narcissistic mutual gaze. What such a violent fantasy has to do with life in a 'hermitage' where unique 'peace' is vested securely is not clear; neither, at least initially, are the unstable grammatical connectives and indeterminate pronouns ('So', 'they'). The violently original eyebeam thrusts aside the comfortable regularities of syntax and perspective.

Later, in the Holy Sonnets, this Mannerist perspective would intimate a visionary glory beyond the copyist's art. Donne's version of 'Jesus wept' has a traumatizing beauty, contracting the conflict of the Passion into one line: 'Teares in his eyes quench the amasing light' (Holy Sonnet XIII, l. 5). 'Amasing' is the stunned word which covers for all that cannot be said by the human witness: acknowledging only awe and wonder, it also conveys a visual afterglare of the unearthly intensity of a light to which the human eye is maladaptive and which can be conducted to us only through an impression of its staggering effect on the witness. Just as, in Tintoretto's painting, *The Presentation of the Virgin*, emphasis falls on the galvanized emotion of the ordinary human witnesses who guide our attention to the inset subject, so 'amasing' is the authenticating word in the sonnet which gives the scene its frisson of Eternity. But the narrative order of the sentence conspires to delay the revelation until it is already over: 'amasing light' is in the accusative and does not reach us until it has been put out. Just as Baroque art concentrated focus on the reactions of the bystander, centring the marginal and displacing the central, giving apparent priority to the eye witness over the event witnessed, and thence increasing the mystery, terror, or majesty of the subject, so Donne envisions the Passion through the emotion of an implied observer. Scriptural events are portrayed enveloped in consciousness; as Ignatian meditation exercises (see Ch. 3 below), they represent the dynamics of the object of meditation-in-the-mind.

But the 'amasing light' is only there to be 'quenched'. The light from Jesus's eyes is all the more amazing for its absence; its destructibility; its conversion to darkness:

> Teares in his eyes quench the amasing light,
> Blood fills his frownes, which from his pierc'd head fell.

'Quench' puts it out like a fire, the agent being the paradox of those tokens of Divine humanity, Christ's tears. God can cry. Donne has shown him nakedly, in the paroxysms of his human sufferings; and for these throes we — the eyewitnesses — cannot atone. If God's tears (his humanity) can eliminate his light (his divinity), then God can, in that fearful moment, cease to exist as God. Donne has recorded the echo of Christ's cry of despair ('My God, my God, why hast thou forsaken me?') in a single line at once so visually stimulating and so defiant of human power to visualize that it seems to condense the whole mystery of the Passion within it. The technique reaches its fullest imaginative range in the dynamics of 'Goodfriday 1613. Riding Westward', with its towering Cross and its absconding eyewitness (see Ch. 3 below).

Strenuous difficulty, it has often been said, is characteristic of Donne's poetry, just as clearly as his living and personal tone of voice. But the two are really one. Their reciprocity may be experienced within the very grammar of the poems. Grammar is a kind of DNA which carries complex traces of identity into the field of the intelligible. Donne's grammar tends towards the Baroque and Mannerist. Of the two modes of grammar available — parataxis (the accumulation of principle clauses linked by *and* or the equivalent) and hypotaxis (a complex grammar of subordination), Donne's more characteristic sentence structures its meanings hypotactically, and often through a shifting, elliptical, and unstable hypotaxis which makes grammatical relations not immediately comprehensible and possibly (even after study) dubious. This practice is by no means the invariable rule, as witness the poems in the *Songs and Sonets*, which are written as songs, obedient to the regular cadencing of lyric verse-form. In, for instance, the beautiful 'Sweetest love, I doe not goe, | For wearinesse of thee', attunement to the tonalities of Elizabethan song affects diction, manner, verse-form and grammar. Diction here is warmly plain and grammar plain-speaking; the impression is of sensitive and cultivated beauty of thought and feeling. The tender philosophy of the closure founds its assurance on fidelity to the regular CDDC rhyme-pattern, which encloses the parted lovers in 'wee' and 'bee', which surround 'sleepe' and 'keepe' in all-but-complete regularity; it insists on a simple grammar of trust:

> But thinke that wee
> Are but turn'd aside to sleepe;
> They who one another keepe
> Alive, ne'r parted bee.

(ll. 37–40)

However, a more characteristic grammar is founded upon a struggle of the particles and connectives in complex sentences, to establish themselves, not precisely in co-operation with one another but with something of the appearance of competition. Subordinate clauses, by being so assertively insisted upon, seem to rise up against the status of the principal clauses, making interventions which stave off the completion of the major clause or generate new and challenging propositions which lead to swerves of logic and internal wranglings within the poem. Parentheses, whether signalled by brackets or not, are common. Frequently a conditional or causal clause may introduce an image or idea so compelling that it seems to trespass into the status of a second subject, eclipsing the principal:

> For if the sinewie thread my braine lets fall
>> Through every part,
> Can tye those parts, and make mee one of all;
> These haires which upward grew, and strength and art
>> Have from a better braine,
> Can better do'it; Except she meant that I
>> By this should know my pain,
> As prisoners then are manacled, when they'are condemn'd to die.

('The Funerall', ll. 9–16)

>> As our blood labours to beget
>>> Spirits, as like soules as it can,
>> Because such fingers need to knit
>>> That subtile knot, which makes us man:
>> So must pure lovers soules descend
>>> T'affections, and to faculties ...

('The Extasie', ll. 61–6)

The 'sinewie thread', the system of nerves which makes for the cohesion of the potentially disintegrative human creature, though governed by the stern double subordinate *for if* into the status of conditionality (*if* dependent on the causal *for*), has such nervous intellectual vitality that it leaps into predominance. We return anticlimatically to the main clause, imputing talismanic power to the wreath of hair ('These haires ...'). From the X-ray vision into a living body we move again into the posthumous future along the Mannerist angle of vision which provides preposterous focus for the poem's fantasy, to a new consideration of the meaning of the wreath, only to break down upon a new subordinate clause of condition, beginning *Except*. The stymied poem staggers on the disruption of its logic and self-assurance. The meaning of the symbol may, it discerns, be the exact opposite of that argued for in the poem up to this moment. Crown becomes manacle; potent king becomes mortified prisoner. The consciousness of the poem encounters the disturbing realm of the indeterminate and illegible. *For if ... which ... Except*: in this progression of conjunctions, each brags its ability to make clear and delicate differentiations of meaning, defining linguistic relationships in a logical hierarchy of values. But paradoxically it signals, with deliberate irony, that all statements whatever belong in the area of problem. The arts of the lawyer, amateur scientist, and schoolman which Donne brings to his poetry do not release the poet from problem: they rededicate him to it.

Analogous processes are at work in the quotation from 'The Extasie': the 'subtile knot, which makes us man', though clearly subordinated by *As*, has an imaginative power which impresses us as a major statement on the human condition, stirring acutely felt queries as to how to 'see' the image. The passage is a near-miracle of *trompe l'œil*. The 'labouring to beget' seems like a raw representation of the sexual act until its object is met by turning the corner into the next line: 'Spirits'. The space anatomized is revealed as inner space, the self-divided individual whose nature requires to be interwoven by a 'knot'. How can the blood have 'fingers' seeking to tie this knot between body and soul? Why would they 'need' to do so? The imagery is absolutely compelling. We are stretched finely between a forensic exploration of human dualism and the image of lovers' fingers exploring the compulsively needed body. 'Us' universalizes to encompass all of us, not just the poem's lovers. The vision is profound and intricate, forcing us to the edge of the imaginable. But, when the hypotaxis draws its amatory conclusion ('So must pure lovers soules descend | T'affections, and to faculties'), there may be a sense of let-down as the poem moves to a conclusion that seems less worthy than the subordinate clauses that carried us there. For this poem has been read by critics as a serious poem of Neo-platonist idealism and as a seduction-poem that parodies this idealism. For myself, I do not know which is the truer reading: such highly wrought brilliance as Donne displays, on a grammar which spirals like a double helix, may be said to tend relentlessly in the direction of self-parody.

Just as strongly as Donne's colloquial diction, his hypotaxis impresses the reader by its air of improvisation, uneven, full of lacunae, fragmentations, ellipses, and frictions. Deep psychological cross-currents seem to play through its complexities; logic progresses, retrogresses, aborts, or digresses. Mixed motives and high cunning become perceptible. In this realm of problem, the not-said or the denied is often intuited behind the decisive articulations which pretend to a clarity and assurance whose brittleness they betray. Compression and ellipsis sometimes have this effect, as in the ambivalent ending of 'The good-morrow' or the overcrowded second stanza of 'A Valediction: of weeping'. Here the clarifying connectives are simply withdrawn, perhaps through lack of space, to leave a kind of passionate gibberish:

> Till thy teares mixt with mine doe overflow
> This world, by waters sent from thee, my heaven dissolved so.

> (ll. 17–18)

Editors[13] have dealt with these extreme condensations by supplying long and prosaic translations into normal English: that is, they refuse the burden of the Baroque, by expanding and amplifying what has been contracted, and normalizing the distraught spasms of articulation into a 'sensible' prose which (ironically) makes Donne's message seem more rather than less absurd. It is the unsettledness of the grammar, its disputability (is *that* an adjective or a conjunction? to what does *it* or *they* or *what* refer?), which sets up an excitement in Donne's rhetorical devices. His appearance of exactitude, subtlety, and richly shaded reasoning often clashes with the obscurity of the linguistic world in which he is at home.

Within this realm of problem, however, there exist passages of extraordinary calm and cogency — the compass image in 'A Valediction: forbidding mourning', the blossoming bough of 'Loves growth' (ll. 19–20) — and an impressive brevity which stands out against the surrounding conflict by abandoning the convolutions of hypotaxis for the naked statement of parataxis:

> My face in thine eye, thine in mine appeares,
> And true plain hearts doe in the faces rest ...

> ('The good-morrow', ll. 15–16)

Not the vexed *but* or *if, because, since* or *for*, but the rare relaxation of *And* links the lines in the peace of a mutual gaze, allowing the lovers to read one another with briefly perfect legibility in the sabbath of a timeless 'rest'.

2

The Male

Donne has been congratulated on writing on behalf of the human race. But this is an illusion. He writes as a male. The confusion between the word 'man' as denoting both 'male' and 'humanity' is germane to our culture, written into the English language and the cultural assumptions it enshrines and perpetuates. The male is privileged as spokes*man* for the tribe. Generations of critics — generally male, or women successful in the patriarchal academic world — have not only failed to locate and anatomize the problems of the sexualized vision Donne puts forward in his poetry but have actively colluded in his fantasies of omnivorous potency, preening their own maleness in the glamorized light in which he (on occasions) gilds viciousness and denies the sublimated problems which are the real and fascinating subjects of certain poems. As an undergraduate in the late 1960s I was told that Donne's 'muscular and powerful' style was 'masculine', in contrast to the more 'feminine' smoothness of the Spenserians: obediently, we all inscribed this wisdom, excited no doubt by the sheer sexuality of the love-poems into an amiable blindness to the deeper implications both of their power and of that of its exponents. The image of Donne in early life as a jaunty, philandering rake is one which a body of his earlier texts, including some of the *Songs and Sonets*, Elegies, and Satires, exhibit with pride: critics have tended either to smirk collusively or to tolerate these literary 'wild oats', sown with such brilliant wit. Latterly John Carey has outdone them all in an otherwise brilliant book by a kind of swashbuckling phallicism: 'We are careful to talk, nowadays, as if we believed the male ought to respect the female's individuality. Donne is above such hypocrisies ...' (Carey, 100). Carey is to be thanked for his self-exposing candour: he clarifies the common assumption that 'we' (man) are all 'men' (males). Misogyny is accepted or applauded by the critical tradition as a performance art. And indeed there is no doubt that Donne does it very well.

I have queried the relationship of biography and poetry, proposing a scepticism appropriate to Donne's own. But one personal fact cannot be dismissed from a reading of his works and that is the fact of gender. Donne himself insisted upon it, referring in Elegie XVI, 'On his Mistris', to his language as a tool of rhetorical impregnation: 'that remorse | Which my words masculine perswasive force | Begot in thee' (ll. 3–5). Eulogists writing to lament Donne's death recorded a comparable view: his powerful innovations and especially his excavations into the riches of the vernacular were regarded as a redemption from the 'feminine' slavery of English poetry to the servile imitations of classicism. Donne, says Thomas Carew, has

> open'd Us a Mine
> Of rich and pregnant phansie, drawne a line
> Of masculine expression ...[1]

Masculine is a term of praise. Carew leads on to celebration of Donne's 'imperious wit' before which 'Our stubborne language bends', as against the classical 'soft melting Phrases' it supplanted (ll. 49, 50, 53). *Masculine* and *feminine* are used as linguistic value-judgments, on the model of the traditional gender-specifications Milton was to formulate so handily in *Paradise Lost*:

> Not equal, as their sex not equal seemd;
> For contemplation hee and valour formd,
> For softness she and sweet attractive Grace ...[2]

Masculine expression would be identifiable as intellectual and commanding, as against the supine deliquescence of the *feminine* 'soft melting Phrases' of the literary tradition. The Spenserian gentleness of late Elizabethan poetry, with its reverence for the ancients and for harmony and lyric beauty, implies to the devotee of Donne an effeminacy (always a term of contempt) because it lacks the phallic thrusting techniques or technologies which can 'open ... us a Mine', with the suggestion of sexual penetration.

Indeed, Donne has himself spoken of the vagina as a mine, into which the phallus deludedly plunged in search of riches in the womb:

> Some that have deeper digg'd loves Myne than I,
> Say, where his centrique happinesse doth lie;
> I have lov'd, and got, and told,
> But should I love, get, tell, till I were old,

> I should not finde that hidden mysterie;
> Oh, 'tis imposture all

('Loves Alchymie', ll. 1–6)

Gold, silver, and diamond-mines were also associated with the New World, raided by the colonialists whose enterprise so caught Donne's imagination: in 'The Sunne Rising', 'both the'India's of spice are Myne' are in the lovers' bed to be enjoyed by him (l. 17). For Donne, sexual possession of the female is characteristically equated with territorial acquisition. She is 'all States, and all Princes, I' (l. 21), though this proprietorial relationship of male ruler to female demesne may on occasion be reformed into a mutual common wealth of precious parity in which they are both, uniquely, Kings of one another in an élite of two ('The Anniversarie', ll. 23–6). More commonly, though, the woman is:

> My kingdome, safeliest when with one man man'd,
> My Myne of precious stones, My Emperie …

(Elegie XIX, 'Going to Bed', ll. 28–9)

The congratulations Donne earned on his *masculinity* of expression are the trophies of a kind of linguistic colonialism which finds virtue in aggression and self-authentication in irreverent rhetorical self-display. It disclaims all forms of obedience, including metrical obedience, as servility. Jonson informed his friend Drummond that 'Done for not keeping of accent deserved hanging' (*Heritage*, 69), the implication being that accent (metrical conformity) was a discipline to which the poet was obliged to bow. But Donne's famous roughness and irregularities of rhythm are a coherent part of his profession of *masculinity* of language. Language is there to be fought and forced, not coaxed and wheedled if one wishes to play the man.

Much of Donne's earlier poetry specializes in obscenity. It was written by a young male bent on establishing a reputation in a male society at Lincoln's Inn, where fraternal bondings and dominance were founded on the sexual prowess (whether real or feigned) of members of a predatory pack. It is not to rebuke the young poet for his supposed bad behaviour that one must stress this favour-currying machismo: rather to reproach collusive criticism for blind praise and to clarify the extent of Donne's misogyny. For traces of that misogyny, founded on fear, anger and insecurity as well as

32

desire for approbation in a patriarchal world, are pervasive in his work. It is paradoxically an aspect of his idealism, and its psychological burdens test his trust, in the most lovely and moving of his love-poems. Misogyny grasps deep roots into the psyche that generates these poems. It is experienced as excruciatingly hurtful to himself and comes away with something like the uncanny shriek of the mandrake root in 'Twicknam Garden', whose 'groan' he records (l. 17), the aphrodisiac with forked roots like legs which was fabled to scream when pulled from the ground. Amongst the profoundest of the love-poems are those which understand that they have brought a lonely, bitter inheritance of poison into the Garden of Love, 'The spider love, which transubstantiates all, | And can convert Manna to gall' (ll. 6–7). Such poems allow us to gaze into the disturbing and disturbed depths of a mind fascinated by the relationship of its own insecurities and fears of rejection to its betrayals and self-betrayals. The sleights and devices of the neurotic levity of the cynical philanderer's lyrics in the *Songs and Sonets* provide an important slant on this vision.

In 'Woman's constancy' Donne attributes his own least lovable characteristics — fickleness, casuistry, vindictive intent — to a woman on whom he rounds ('Vaine lunatique ...', l. 14) to threaten payment in kind; in 'Communitie', he elaborates a poker-faced theology of male promiscuity, which bursts out into a triumphant definition of woman as consumable commodity, for arbitrary use:

> Chang'd loves are but chang'd sorts of meat,
> And when hee hath the kernell eate,
> Who doth not fling away the shell?

(ll. 22–4)

In 'Confined Love' he condemns the law of monogamy as the fabrication of the impotent; in 'Loves Alchymie' he advises, 'Hope not for minde in women' (l. 23), for they are no better than animated corpses; in 'Loves diet' he develops a metaphor from falconry which permits him to 'spring a mistresse', go through the amatory motions, 'And the game kill'd, or lost, goe talke, and sleepe' (ll. 29–30). There is a strong background of male community to this poem, both in the sporting image and the echo of social talk. 'Farewell to love' reflects upon post-coital torpor and 'The Indifferent' wittily brags its promiscuity, where humorous cynicism yields to the aggressive questions of the second stanza, with its savage slur on women's mothers (l. 11), implying deeper levels of Hamlet-like anxiety in the speaker. In 'Loves Usury' he celebrates male rapacity and the stealth of indecent games with women's attachments in a bargain which will 'let I Mee travell, sojourne, snatch, plot, have, forget, I Resume my last yeares relict' (ll. 4–6). The mischief-making verbs and the callously transgressive indifference to the feelings of the cast-off are matched in the second stanza by the frenchified 'comfitures of Court, I Or cities quelque choses'. Wiles of Don Juanesque syntax and the knowing winks of clique diction solicit the reader to join or envy the insolent subculture of youthful males.

The stated intent of such poems is the dehumanization of woman. She becomes an edible commodity; usable goods which, when sampled, are rendered worthless; game to be flushed out and killed; a mindless piece of flesh without individuality, whose feelings are expressly not to be taken into account: 'I can love her, and her, and you and you' ('The Indifferent', l. 8). Having no ethical qualities, she is a born man-trap: 'No where I Lives a woman true and faire' ('Song: Goe, and catche a falling starre', ll. 17–18). All Donne's poems have male speakers, except two: 'Breake of Day', in which a woman grumbles at her lover's eagerness to get up and be about his business, and 'Sapho to Philaenis', a lesbian fantasy. This *jeu d'esprit* imagines the poet Sappho admiring her naked body in a mirror and identifying her own reflection narcissistically with her lover, Philaenis. The poem is in part a masturbatory fantasy, comparable with several of Donne's Elegies, in which 'touching my selfe, all seemes done to thee' (l. 52), and witty rejection is made of the bristly hairiness of male lovers (l. 33) and of their calling-card, the semen, which 'the tillage of a harsh rough man' leaves behind (l. 38), as against the secret and unsignified embrace between woman and woman (ll. 39–42). Narcissism, always a preoccupation of Donne, is here at the core of his sexual fantasy; the female 'I' which represents the consciousness of the poem evinces a humorous sympathy for Sappho's frustrated longings which makes the poem more — just a little more — than a titillating exercise. This act of impersonation is so rare as to point up the fact that Donne's poetry, despite its quality of immediate dialogue with an unseen, unheard other, is not as genuinely 'dramatic' as it is usually said to be. Its elements of detailed scene-setting I should rather describe as 'fantasy'. For a central factor in dramatic writing — characterization — is all but lacking in Donne's work. Whereas in Browning's aptly-styled 'dramatic monologues', impersonation implies a world of social and personal relations to which the individuals (each novelistically odd and distinct) belong, Donne's poetry presents, not character in a dramatic situation but the theatrical ego on a private stage, whose player and audience are equally the self. That ego experiences and presents itself as masculine: its problems and project are those of maleness, and its gender is antecedent to its intellectual, theological, and scientific interests.

The Elegies display the male persona's potency in a series of libertine, epigrammatic, and sometimes narrative exercises written 'for the boys', each more outrageous than the last. 'The boys' are the brothel-going, cuckolding, big-talking fraternity, or at least those who exhibit themselves in these terms, and who at the same time like to identify themselves as an *avant-garde* intelligentsia. The fantasy scenarios of the Elegies convulse with lurid detail, from the encrusted vomiting body of the husband imagined as poisoned by the adulterous woman in 'Jealosie' (Elegie I) to the ironic praise of the repulsive woman in 'The Anagram' (Elegie II), whom ultimately even 'Dildoes, Bedstaves and her Velvet Glasse' avoid touching (l. 53). In 'Change', with its profane erotic use of theological terms, Donne expresses fear of the 'hot, wily, wild' and bestially promiscuous nature of woman (l. 12), praising philandering as the way to refresh stagnant waters: 'Waters stincke soone, if in one place they bide' (l. 31). His 'yet much, much I feare thee' (l. 4) speaks volumes about the anxiety underlying the misogynist posture. In Elegie VII ('Natures lay Ideot ...') fear of female autonomy is expressed in a fantasy of a woman who uses the sexual sophistication acquired from the persona to subvert his possession. 'Strangers taste' the knowledge he planted, and the colt he has broken is a horse for many riders (l. 30). Here the confederacy of fellow males is viewed with suspicion as a pack of rivals competing for sexual access. In 'The Comparison' (Elegie VIII) a revolting contrast is drawn between 'my Mistris' and a stinking, sweating whore, whose physical characteristics are compared with boils, scum, warts, carcases, gout. Rank sexual horror and a perverse pleasure in that horror inform the tone. The pudenda are described in terms of gunpowder explosions and a lava-singed volcano:

> Thine's like the dread mouth of a fired gunne,
> Or like hot liquid metalls newly runne

Into clay moulds, or like to Ætna
Where round about the grasse is burnt away.

(ll. 39–42).

This sick poem culminates in imagery of probing a wound, a conception whose psychopathology deserves deeper exploration. Amongst this tasteless brew are cited exceptions like 'The Autumnall' (Elegie IX), a witty eulogy of Mrs Herbert, conveying some tenderness; 'His parting from her' (Elegie XII), a chiaroscuro self-dramatizing valedictory; the vivid fantasy, 'On his Mistris' (Elegie XVI). But the norm is set by the insulting 'Julia' (Elegie XIII); the witty narrative, 'A Tale of a Citizen and his Wife' (Elegie XIV) with its conspiracy between the virile young narrator and the nubile wife against her husband, a garrulous old geyser complaining of the modern world, climaxing at the underhand assignation of the final line (l. 71). Elegie XVII ('Variety') is a libertine's charter, written as an academic exercise arguing from the law of nature and the sexual freedom of the Golden Age; 'Loves Progress' (Elegie XVIII) proposes that the 'right true end' of love (l. 2) is to get down the hole of the female genitals (l. 32). Global navigation of woman's anatomy accords ultimate priority to the pudenda, the second and more desirable of woman's 'Two purses' (l. 92), the other being the mouth. Elegie XIX, 'Going to Bed', is an erotic command-performance which ordains a female strip-tease on a scintillating logic of *double entrendre*. 'Loves Warre' (Elegie XX) forswears the warrior-profession in favour of sexual combat: 'Here let me parlee, batter, bleede, and dye' (l. 30), with the familiar Renaissance cant pun on 'bleede and dye' for ejaculation.

I have relentlessly, prosaically, and in a style which no doubt betrays a certain distaste, laid out the subjects of the Elegies in a killjoy fashion. These poems are generally hailed or dismissed as juicy juvenilia, praised for their intellectual brilliance and poetic panache; then subordinated to the 'great' poetry of Donne — in a sense, suppressed. But not only do they form a considerable bulk of his poetic output; they are foundation-stones for his mature poetry. Establishing an ideology, they expose the symptoms of a male aggression and exploitativeness as a mode of defiance against society as a gerontocracy, sanctioned by his peers and licensed by his dominance of wit and Ovidian shock-tactics. They attack convention as castrated and sapless, dishonourable because dishonest. The poet advertises himself as a fully equipped male. Other poets may offer compliments, flattery, sweet similitudes; he presents a naked priapism and brags thereby his dangerous integrity.

However, in so doing, he leaves himself vulnerably open. The profoundest of the *Songs and Sonets* are conscious of this vulnerability: their struggle is with and in it. The Elegies, less conscious, are more crudely revelatory of complexes suffered by the male, even in the act of self-delighting fantasy. Such fantasy pervades the collection, which promotes to an art-form the low-grade means of imaginative self-arousal. In 'The Perfume', sexual fantasy is stimulated by thrilled guilt at the thought of being snooped on as the persona furtively enjoys his mistress in a family household. The girl's father is 'thy Hydroptique father' (l. 6); the mother, 'thy immortall mother' (l. 13), ferreting about for signs of her daughter's lust; the tell-tale little brothers (l. 27) scamper in and out of the bedroom; and, finally, 'The grim eight-foot-high iron-bound serving-man', on a scale with the Rhodian Colossus (ll. 31–4), is a paid informer. This detail, with its grotesque distortion of human proportion, swells into the realm of the hallucinatory and inaugurates the bizarre dimensions of a world where silks are dissuaded from whistling and 'opprest shoes' (an image drawn from pressing-to-death by torture) (ll. 51–2) have no tongues. Such wild antics of the fantasy recur in every poem, from the self-fascinated image of the bag of bones, pock-marked with gunpowder, who is imagined returning from his voyage in 'His Picture' (Elegie V) to the sodomitical fantasies of the racist and queasily homoerotic 'On his Mistris' (Elegie XVI), in which Italian inverts will take advantage of his girlfriend should she decide to follow him to war dressed as a page-boy (ll. 38–41). The subject of 'His Picture' (his farewell-gift of a portrait of himself) is eclipsed by the grotesque auto-voyeurism of the transformed 'weather-beaten' man (l. 5) he fantasizes as returning to travesty the picture of the title. Voyeurism, and especially espionage on the self and its future or possible postures, is a constant obsession of Donne's work. Peeping Toms are everywhere, even in the sanctum of 'The Extasie' (ll. 21–8, 73–6).

If Donne views the female sexual organs as a 'purse', a 'mine', or a kind of wound, he exposes a symptomatology of his own. He bares a mental wound which is cultural and mass produced and, rather than particular to Donne, endemic to 'civilization'. John Carey's admiration for the similitudes that crown Elegie VIII ('The Comparison') brings this into shocking relief. Congratulating the poet on the 'success' of the 'sensitizing' effect achieved by the 'implicit notion of copulating with a hot gun barrel', he goes on to quote the concluding section, which praises the insertion of phallus into vagina as a priest's evisceration or the insertion of a surgeon's probe:

> so devoutly nice
> Are Priests in handling reverent sacrifice,
> And such in searching wounds the Surgeon is
> As wee, when wee embrace, or touch, or kisse.

(ll. 49–52)

The 'painful connotations of the comparison', says Carey, 'mingle with a sense of infinitely gentle and caring penetration which both surgeon and lover are engaged on ... Donne achieves his enlivening effect by ... the intrusion of blunt metal among the most shrinkingly sensitive living tissues' (Carey, 142). So indeed, does pornography. Carey shares the unquestioned assumptions that underlie Donne's male fantasy-world: that a phallus is somehow a tool; a vagina a wound. English sexual idiom itself is forged from this objectification of the male organ and depersonalization of the female body. 'Draw thy tool', says Gregory in *Romeo and Juliet*, after a thirty-line verbal bout equating phallus with sword. 'My naked weapon is out', replies Samson (I. i. 36, 38). Donne's poem represents sex first as a holy disembowelling, with the male performing the priestly rites (ll. 49–50); then as the equally authoritative and curative action of a surgeon on a patient. In each case the woman is by implication helpless, supine, exposed, invaded.

Women readers may doubt the 'healing efficacy' of such interventions (Carey, 143) on the grounds that we are anatomically sound in the first place. But the male critic in this instance is too aroused to address such issues. Carey goes on to quote an analogy in the 'Epithalamion made at Lincolnes Inn', which he admits worries him a little more. The bride, having been put to bed,

> at the Bridegroomes wish'd approach doth lye
> Like an appointed lambe, when tenderly
> The priest comes on his knees t'embowel her.

(ll. 88-90)

The idea of ripping out guts through the tender sexual parts inspires Carey to fantasize on the lamb's bowels landing in a soft heap on the floor and the sexual sacrificer straddling towards his 'girl' on his knees, weapon erect. He invokes poetic technique as a way of rendering this obscenity respectable. Such images intensify 'the body's vulnerability by bringing it up against something hard and instrumental' (Carey, 144). Here the dishonesty of the reading comes into full focus, for it is not 'the body's' but the 'female body's' vulnerability that is intensified. Donne is opening the legs of a woman to the hard and instrumental gaze of the male voyeur and inviting a subtle version of a gross gratification. In 'Going to Bed', he would instruct 'As liberally, as to a Midwife, shew I Thy self' (ll. 44-5). The reader's eyes are directed invasively to the private parts of the woman addressed, through the false sanction of an image which offers a protective agency: doctor, surgeon, midwife. The humour and ingenuity of the sequence (which condemns feminist objection as prudish and dull-witted) is another aspect of this false sanction.

Contempt for women remains a major theme of the *Songs and Sonets*, which span a range of amatory poetry from the salacious and abusive to the tender and passionate. Why then should women readers come to Donne at all? For brilliance of poetic technique is not enough to justify obscene ideology; an insult remains an insult. George Parfitt's admirable short study of Donne provides a worthwhile answer when he suggests that the poetry 'may be of value to women because it is so revealing of the male, and to men ... because it tells disturbing truth of men.'[3] Another answer would be to divert attention to Donne's unique capacity to express mutual sensuous joy, in poems like 'The good-morrow', 'The Sunne Rising', 'The Anniversarie'; the sharp interrogatives of desire which glorify the loved ones of 'Aire and Angels' into 'Some lovely glorious nothing', the shake of her hair an example of 'things I Extreme, and scatt'ring bright' (ll. 6, 22). For the phallic probe or knife of the offensive elegy, the tender eroticism of 'Loves growth' could be substituted:

> Gentle love deeds, as blossomes on a bough,
> From loves awakened root do bud out now.

(ll. 19–20)

In this rare nature image, the 'awakened root' while clearly phallic in implication exploits nobody; it engenders cherishing acts ('Gentle love deeds'), seasonably and reciprocally. But this emphasis would be an evasion. I hope to demonstrate that some of the profundity of the *Songs and Sonets* comes of their acknowledgement of those primitive and irrational terrors of woman which nourish, on the one hand, violent and insulting male attitudes and, on the other, insecurity, dependence, and possessiveness. Donne probes this wound, epitomized in the admission in Elegie III ('Change'); 'yet much, much I feare thee' (l. 4). The *Songs and Sonets* dialectically assert two opposite principles, which are the Siamese twins bred by a single condition: (1) 'I cannot trust you and therefore I shall scorn and use you', and (2) 'I must possess you totally because my life depends upon you; but I fear I shall lose you'. The techniques by which he seeks to assert control over his fears include the device familiar throughout his life's work, from the Elegies to the Holy Sonnets: the imperative verb. The love poems urge, command, demand, argue, or vehemently asseverate, playing a confident surface of definition and logical demonstration over depths of insecurity or panic. The craving for superiority or supremacy which claims royal power and possession – 'Princes doe but play us' ('The Sunne Rising', l. 23); 'We'are Kings' ('The Anniversarie', l. 23) – is undermined by pathological insecurity which has no sooner dazzled itself with the image of power than it is contemplating the treason that scourges kingship ('The Anniversarie', ll. 25–6), with which it deals through the strategy of denial. Supernatural status is claimed (the Phoenix of 'The Canonization') to stave off the dismaying possibility of being found, after all, banal. Eternal love is located over an abyss of prospective loss; a vaunting tone expresses dire lack of safety; the realm of romantic ideality (two faithful lovers in the one tomb) exists literally and literarily above the realm of savage cynicism:

> When my grave is broke up againe
> Some second ghest to entertaine,
> > (For graves have learn'd that woman-head
> > To be to more than one a Bed)
> > And he that digs it, spies
> A bracelet of bright haire about the bone,
> > Will he not let'us alone ...

('The Relique', 1–7)

The grating parenthesis, signalling a neurotic leap to flippant sexual jest, has a quality both edgily digressive and nervously to the point. Just as the grave is 'broke up', so buried psychological contents irrupt incontinently through the broken surface of the tone and invade the syntactic progression by adding a secondary to a secondary clause, delaying the main clause.The misogynistic quip is in blackly farcical conflict with the ensuing glory of the 'bracelet of bright haire about the bone'. No coherent link is offered between parenthesis and context. A more sensible poet would have deleted it in a second draft. But for Donne, making sense is not the priority. The very absence of rationality here presents a psychological truth which Donne's poetry incomparably articulates: the impossible conflicts and burdens of the male mind all but eviscerated by its inheritance, which makes its neuroses and stratagems its own subject.

The troubled psyche is the field of study in 'Twicknam Garden' ('take my teares' (l. 20)) and 'A nocturnall upon S. Lucies Day' ('Study me then ...' (l. 10)). The burden of a darkened, riven mind is brought within the focus of his wit, which acts like an optical instrument of ingenious construction to anatomize contents hidden from normal, unaided vision. Refracted light, in these *trompe l'œil* mental experiments, sees us round corners to glimpse the profoundest reaches of a manipulative and self-manipulating brain. 'Twicknam Garden' originates in the search for mental health. But the sufferer is chronically incapable of restoring himself in the medicinal garden since he is constrained to invade it with his own violently sick presence. Lady Bedford's privileged park receives the visitation of a turbulent, damaged presence whose proudly self-mocking tone records the infiltration of an outsider into the well-endowed inside-world:

> Blasted with sighs, and surrounded with teares,
>> Hither I come to seeke the spring,
>> And at mine eyes, and at mine eares,
> Receive such balmes, as else cure every thing;
>> But O, selfe traytor, I do bring
> The spider love, which transubstantiates all,
>> And can convert Manna to gall,
> And that this place may thoroughly be thought
>> True Paradise, I have the serpent brought.

(ll. 1–9)

Hellish desperation, full of impotent violence, is artfully shaped
and mythologized into an epic event of Biblical status; a sinister,
arachnid presence consumes the picturesque view which it digests
into the poisonous stuff of his own subjectivity, an act of
sacrilegious 'transubstantiation'; its bale introduces a contaminant
to this latter-day Eden, demonically linked with the Serpent as arch-
destroyer. The mirthlessly self-mocking tone speaks of a trauma-
tized state of mind that can see and desire sanity and balance but
cannot relax into health. The persona of 'Twicknam Garden'
dramatizes himself as a spirit of rapacity with no power to enact his
despoiling urges, which hence turn against himself. Like the
suffering Mephostophilis of *Dr Faustus* or Milton's Lucifer, the
estranged figure of Donne's poem carries an aura of damnation, not
without its own furtive glamour.

The first stanza's refusal to disclose to us the source of its
affliction rather intensifies than weakens the impression of a
pathological state of mind, whose introspection is a factor in the
disease. What is the matter with him? He does not say. The poem
neither divulges nor ponders the circumstances which precipitated
its hellbent urgency, at least until the final stanza, when sexual
rejection is introduced as its pretext, but the concluding misogy-
nistic outburst (ll. 24–7) supplies not the cause but a further set of
symptoms. The persona's state of mind is laid out for anatomiza-
tion. The second stanza, with its excruciated flinching from the
ironic 'glory' of the springtime garden (l. 11), develops the sense of
a mind so estranged that the external world is perceived as its
enemy. The trees that 'laugh, and mocke mee to my face' (l. 13)
reinforce the bitterness of exclusion, parodying the stock Petrarchan
situation of the rejected lover mocked by a sylvan or pastoral scene,
and at the same time adapting it to a theatre for the maladaptive
ego to display its injury. Only by deadening his quick responses
could he find refuge in the mocking garden: hence the turn in
Stanza II in which he imagines incorporation as an insentient part
of the garden's horticulture and architecture: as a mandrake, with
its sinister and aphrodisiac potency, or a 'stone fountain weeping
out my yeare' (l. 18). Twicknam Park, a formal, geometrical garden
set out in around 1609 to the most modern specifications but in the
circular plan of the pre-Copernican universe, inset into squares, was
a symbol of the aristocratic status quo. Donne, Lady Bedford's
hanger-on, seeks admission to a closed universe which has no place

for him. Biography in this instance may shed a little hypothetical light on the angry humiliation of the poem's emotion. The titled world closes ranks against him, for socially he has no right or function there save to amuse Lady Bedford with his poetic ingenuity; hence, perhaps, the emphasis on 'disgrace' (l. 14) as the parvenu curries favour with a powerful woman to whom he scorns to bend and yet before whom he has abased himself before and will again.

The desire to become a 'stone fountain' would hardly occur to everyone. By such resort he abdicates the sombre and excoriated mockery of the earlier lines for a more stylized and mannered conceit, which issues the invitation to lovers to queue with their lachrymatories and carry home his bottled tears to be sampled and compared for quality with their mistresses'. He flaunts his distress as that of an élite sensitivity. By demotion to the status of an inanimate functionary, the fountain, he promotes himself to the status of arbiter and centralized symbol. Metamorphosed into the unfeeling symbol of his all-too-feeling self, he will at once penetrate the grounds of the Establishment and (though personally frustrated) dominate the social scene by the authenticity of his incomparable texts. The 'teares, which are loves wine' of the final stanza surely represent the poems, in which he distils his sense of rejection, just as the 'well wrought urne' of 'The Canonization' refers to the exquisitely shaped vessel of the poem, which not only compensates for the unavailability of the 'half-acre tombes' of the great (ll. 33–4) but reveals their essential vulgarity and vanity. The mortuary image, self-commemorating, self-mourning, represents love-poetry, which becomes a kind of epitaph in the moment of completion. The stone fountain is an important focus of the exhibitionistically eccentric self-therapy of 'Twicknam Garden'. In an age of novelties, when the revived science of hydraulics had been applied to garden architecture on a grand scale, initiating speaking statues, water organs, tweeting birds, mobile sculptures, and any number of automata, ingenious simulacra adorned the newfangled gardens of the rich. The garden was an artificial environment planned to glorify the owner within a symbolic political and cosmic order. Donne fantasizes a role as an automaton, a statue of himself through which a merely emblematic and exemplary water flows. Such tears do not scald, because their stone conduit is dead to pain. The anodyne suggestions of this image are therapeutic, because they locate the sufferer in the art-world, where water pressure can be raised *ad absurdum* without ill effect. This mock-petrification opens the way to the retaliatory generalization in the final quatrain: 'O perverse sexe, where none is true but shee ...' (l. 26), which softens the special horror of social or sexual rejection and oblique 'disgrace'. He may have brought the Serpent into the garden, but Eve is landed with the blame. The consciousness of the poem is stable and acute enough to know, mock and rue its own instability. Resting on the strong metrical foundations of its nine-line pentameters, the poem's composing mind comprehends its self-betrayals, wry and detached.

'A nocturnall upon S. Lucies Day' is also associated with Lucy Harington, though not directly, for she did not die until 1627, long after Donne is thought to have composed the poem. Here a forensic act of introspection meditates a state of mind more profoundly dark than 'Twicknam Garden', but related to it. As final catastrophe is to danger, so the 'nocturnall' is to 'Twicknam Garden'. Sombre passion combines with slow pace to create an impression of grave, scathed dignity which raises elegy to the level of requiem. Chiasmus encompasses its circular structure, which begins and ends in the Winter Solstice, the shortest day and longest night of the calendar. The first line, 'Tis the yeares midnight, and it is the dayes', is repeated and reversed in the last, 'this | Both the yeares, and the dayes deep midnight is'. The circle seals us into the stasis of mourning, the apparently endless vigil to which the bereaved are committed, unable to move, or to wish to move, into a future without the beloved person. The heavily stressed, measured monosyllables of the repeated and conclusive 'dáyes déep mídnight ís' retard the speaking voice to a *lento* or *adagio* tempo. Constrained to a majestic rhythm, the simple diction condemns the reader to prolong the vigilant act of witness. The lyric voice attains an epic dignity in a poem which commemorates what it elegizes. Who then was Lucy? It is meaningless to say that she was Donne's patron and, secondarily, the name he gave to one of his daughters, no doubt as a way of recommending himself to Lady Bedford. For 'Lucy' in the poem is *lux*, light, darkly focused in a poem of tenebrous shadow, which is a testament of darkness and the experience of non-being. Lucy is a time (13 December) subject to endless recurrence; a place (the landscape of the first stanza); an archetype of loss; the experience of *anomie* or ontological draining, before which words fail and within which human beings stand isolated, incommunicado:

> Tis the yeares midnight, and it is the dayes,
> *Lucies*, who scarce seaven houres herself unmaskes,
>   The Sunne is spent, and now his flasks
>   Send forth light squibs, no constant rayes;
>   The worlds whole sap is sunke:
> The generall balme th'hydroptique earth hath drunk,
> Whither, as to the beds-feet, life is shrunke,
> Dead and enterr'd; yet all these seeme to laugh,
> Compar'd with mee, who am their Epitaph.

(ll. 1–9)

Such desperate trouble is commonly signalled through clinical technical terms, of which 'depression' seems the least unsatisfactory, with its implication of going 'low', being 'down', which the 'nocturnall' literalizes in its focus on the sun's burial, the sap's sinking, the gravewards direction of mind and body. In this universal *nox, nihil, nichts, néant* of bereavement, the poet has a sole advantage over fellow-sufferers: where our dismay is speechless (and that is part of our trauma), he can speak.

Here, if anywhere, the 'I' of the poem is registered as human before it is male: all readers may identify with it. Yet this 'I' is still speaking from a psychic distress intrinsic to the constellation of masculine and acculturated needs discussed earlier. Terror of separation from one on whom he depends charges Donne's lyrics with apprehension or resentment, motivates their stratagems, or brings out the tender empathy that reassures his lover in 'A Valediction: forbidding mourning'. It bred the consolation of compound verbs signifying the joining of the two sundered lovers who are 'Inter-assured of the mind' (1. 19); or whose hands are 'entergraft[ed]' and souls 'interinanimate[d]' in 'The Extasie' (ll. 9, 42). In the latter poem, the enemy to human happiness is the fact of being born single and individual, inheriting 'Defects of lonelinesse' (l. 44), a resonant phrase to convey the shadow-side of Donne's boastful uniqueness. The dissident individual is also the solitary. These contradictory compulsions towards singularity and towards incorporation in and with the beloved other play dialectically through the poetry. When union occurs, it becomes a new kind of singularity, defined against the crowd of *hoi poloi* who inhabit the rest of the world: the 'Dull sublunary lovers' of 'A Valediction:

forbidding mourning; (l. 13), the 'Weake men' of 'The Extasie' (l. 70). In such incorporations, sex paradoxically annuls sexual distinctions, since the other is converted into the substance of the self. As 'the'Eagle and the Dove' and 'The Phoenix', the lovers of 'The Canonization' (ll. 22, 23) unite their opposite qualities in an androgynous whole. 'Wee in us' (that is, both and each in a new 'us' indistinguishably compounded of the two) have mysteriously abolished gender: 'So to one neutrall thing both sexes fit' (l. 25). The verb 'fit' expresses the conjunction of the sexual organs in an act which converts them, in their very chemistry, to an hermaphrodite, which the alchemists used as a figure for a stage in the process towards perfection (*conjunctio*), and Hermetic mysticism (for which there was a Renaissance vogue) associated with the creativity of a bisexual God. In copulation, 'either sex infuses itself into the other ... the female acquires masculine vigour, and the male is relaxed in feminine languour'.[4] Donne, so concerned with secrets and arcane knowledge, draws abundantly on occultism to reinforce his presentation of a carnality that is spiritually 'mysterious' not despite but because of its enactment through the genital organs, which, fitting one another literally, beget a new and impersonal 'us': 'one neutrall *thing*' (emphasis added). To use sex to transcend sex is to 'forget the Hee and Shee' in an occult art which should be hidden (he reveals) from the profane ('The undertaking', l. 20). Alchemy, sneered at as charlatanism in many poems, becomes a guiding metaphor in the 'nocturnall'.

But here the alchemical process has been thrown, by the death of the beloved, into reverse. From golden perfection, the world degrades to its base constituents, and nightmarishly regresses again to the chaos or nothing which preceded creation, and back again, to the quintessence of that chaos or nothing. The identification with another as an *alter ego* who is necessary and intrinsic to the soul's survival, in embracing dependence as safety, also opens the lover to the possibility of irreparable loss. In 'The Dissolution' and 'A Feaver' he fingers the wound, extending it into the fiction that the woman constitutes not only his but 'the worlds soule', vacating a reality which recrudesces into a carcass ('A Feaver', ll. 9, 10), a theme which recurs with varying degrees of gravity and levity through the *Songs and Sonets*, his letters ('Your going away hath made London a dead carkasse' (Bald, 186)) and the 'Anniversaries'. The fixation — most movingly explored in the 'nocturnall' — corresponds to the uncanny sense of identification focused in Emily Brontë's treatment of the *alter ego* in *Wuthering Heights*: under the stress of loss, 'the Universe would turn to a mighty stranger. I should not seem a part of it' (Ch. IX). Donne looks the mighty stranger in the face. The mourner, knowing himself to have survived but at the spiritually terminal cost of a perished sense of self, stands in the shadow of existential paradox. The self has spun into a vortex of nihilism and disintegration, in a world whose mass, solidity, weight, and proportion have been forfeit. It is a spectral presence in the midst of incoherence. Yet the poem is impressive precisely because it has not disintegrated. Its foundations, even stronger than those of 'Twicknam Garden', are ironically so adamant that they build articulate form and structure into the experience of formlessness. Ironically again, the first and last words are parts of the verb *to be* — 'Tis' and 'is' — encircling the experience of not-being. Donne presents himself as a chemical experiment upon which Love carried out a new variation upon an ancient scientific procedure:

> For his art did expresse
> A quintessence even from nothingnesse,
> From dull privations, and leane emptinesse:
> He ruin's mee, and I am re-begot
> Of absence, darknesse, death; things which are not.

(ll. 14–18)

Existential horror is accompanied by a fascinated intellectualizing and measured articulation of the absurd but actual state of simultaneous being and non-being. The subjective is objectivized. But the passionate intelligence of this night-poem, rigorously structured upon the condensed logic of its abstruse metaphor, has a power to move the reader which is hauntingly independent of full intellectual understanding. Readers are gripped at a primary level by the tolling of rhythm and repetition: 'All ... all ... all'; 'nothingnesse ... nothing ... nothing ... are not'; 'absence ... absence'; 'Dead ... dead', 'darkness ... shadow'.

This capacity to infuse into difficult and challenging argument phatic tonal qualities which speak intimately, tenderly, or passionately before the reader's mind has fully comprehended the logic, also characterizes 'A Valediction: forbidding mourning'. The poem's message of steadying reassurance is conveyed by the measured steadiness of its metrical composition in octosyllabic quatrains. Though the 'Valediction' rests upon a framework of complex logical argument, signalled by subordinate clauses of concession, condition, and cause ('As ... So ... But ... therefore ... if'), the poem has the quality of quietly intense personal message, which we seem to 'overhear' with a soft shock of emotion at the tender thoughtfulness of the voice. The speaker literally takes thought for the one he leaves behind; makes provision for her. This intelligent voice implies an equally intelligent listener (and indeed there is no pointer in the poem to specify the speaker's gender: *we* supply the 'he' or 'she' by wanting to assume that it is a personal poem). The poem addresses itself primarily to 'us': 'Our two soules ... which are one' (l. 21). We are at the furthest remove from the aspersions of 'Loves Alchymie': 'Hope not for minde in women ...' (l. 23). The 'Valediction' posits a shared philosophic mind, capable of infinite expansion, unconfined to place or sexuality ('eyes, lips, and hands') (l. 20)). The poem inhabits a kind of mental or inner space whose dilations, expansions, and measurements incline away from the hypothetical basis in 'real' time and space. This mental space is an alternative to the familiar locality inhabited by that consensus of the human race (minus two) scorned as 'the layetie', voyeurs who profane the private realm of the transmitted message. This characteristic insistence on the élite (here, priestly) status of the lovers, set against 'Dull sublunary lovers' (l. 13), grounded in flesh, heightens our sense of licit trespass into a private area of communication. In one sense, the poem forbidding mourning also forbids us participation, as members of that excluded 'layetie'; in another, it publicly solicits witness of its secrets by advertising its privacy; and as, in the act of reading, we appropriate its pronoun 'we', it permits us the illusion of initiated status.

The private space the poem inhabits moves on a fluctuating eyeline which is not only relativistic in the Baroque sense but pure of any bearings or co-ordinates, until the famous compass image in the last three stanzas supplies an instrument of measurement able to give dimension to the lovers' created mutual world. Until then, space is neither here nor there. The poem's first location is a room, but this enclosure does not seem to be a room which the lovers have inhabited, or ever will. It stands as an antechamber to the poem, parabolic to it. But we do not know that when, innocent of direction, we first enter:

As virtuous men passe mildly away,
   And whisper to their soules, to goe,
While some of their sad friends doe say,
   The breath goes now, and some say, no ...

(ll. 1–4)

The dramatic vignette introduces us not only to a departure but also to an ethical realm where tact and courtesy attain moral grandeur. The truly 'virtuous' wish even *in extremis* for the comfort of their vigilant friends. The invocation of *virtue* colours the whole of the poem: it carries over into the refusal of hysteria and hyperbole ('teare-floods ... sigh-tempests') and the elaboration of a far more inflated and cosmic hyperbole which is *innocent* (l. 12); into the image of gold as the alchemically perfectly tempered metal, with its connotations of spiritual value; into the *just* motion of the compass-foot, grounded in the 'fixed foot' (l. 35), like the universe upon its axis. In establishing the semblance of an ethical space, the first digressive stanza also concisely introduces an eavesdropping situation. In the hushed, doubtful atmosphere of the death-bed scene, the dying man is himself an eavesdropper on his friends' solicitous conversation ('The breath goes now ... no'), whilst at the same time representing the most private communication of all, as he whispers to himself. Overhearing his silent 'whisper' as he lies incommunicado at the centre of this subdued but climactic drama, the reader is privileged with breathless insight. If the parting of lovers resembles the catastrophe of death, the final integrity of the dying in their care for those who care for the dying may be transferred to the lovers in their separation.

The first stanza is left forever in suspension, its alignment to the next eight stanzas oblique: a subordinate clause only, a mere similitude. But its resonance is unforgettable, raising it to a kind of hallucinatory second subject. From this enclosed room, the imagination conjures itself out, on the stepping-stone of the scorned earthquakes and tear-floods of Petrarchan convention, to the farthest reach of the cosmos, the 'trepidation of the spheares', the crystalline sphere which was supposed imperceptibly to move all the spheres within it. The entire cosmos, in the unknowable perfection of its architecture and the rarefication of its atmosphere, is now the domain of the lovers' souls. But that totality is also inner space, the contents of the global mind, which, journeying in any direction, never knows 'Absence' because it is not fettered to 'sense' (the senses). That independence, signalled by the tactful pun, does not however wholly refuse or deny the burden of separation. If the poem's lovers care 'lesse' than others about sensory deprivation, it is not to be supposed that they do not care at all. The scientific term 'trepidation' also carries a burden of apprehension. The profound necessity of consolation is demonstrated by the ingenious elaboration of hyperbole into the appearance of an abiding philosophy. But the foundation of the poem's power to persuade is less the cogency of its logic (which swerves at the concession of Stanza VII: 'If they be two ...') than the sense it communicates of personal solicitude, engaging all its intellectual powers in an act of calming reassurance. In the end, the speaker will be able to leave behind him only a provision of words, a testamentary bridge over the abyss of parting as frail as the credibility of whatever images he can conjure out of nothing. While the refined extension of 'gold to ayery thinnesse beate' (l. 24) may intrigue and touch the heart of the person addressed, such airy thinness is unfulfilling. There is an audacious integrity in Donne's willingness to abdicate imagery or argument in favour of new stratagems. For perhaps, ultimately, there is no union. In that case there is temporary division:

> If they be two, they are two so
>   As stiffe twin compasses are two,
> Thy soule the fixt foot, makes no show
>   To move, but doth, if the'other doe.
>
> And though it in the centre sit,
>   Yet when the other far doth rome,
> It leanes, and hearkens after it
>   And growes erect, as that comes home.
>
> Such wilt thou be to mee, who must
>   Like th'other foot, obliquely runne;
> Thy firmnes makes my circle just,
>   And makes me end, where I begunne.

(ll. 25–36)

The compasses of God which circumscribed the creation (Prov. 8: 27); the mathematician's compasses with their cold metallic rigour are appropriate to the poet's loving hand, which releases them from their instrumentality and makes them, if not agents of their own destiny, yet agents of emotion which incline back to their original union. The verbs 'sit ... rome ... leanes ... hearkens' give a human and endeared dimension to the precisely observed action of the compasses, whose destination is 'home'.

If it was possible for Donne to 'forget the Hee and Shee' in erotic poetry, the Divine Poems moved him on to a more transcendent realm of sexual paradox, in which, abdicating his male gender though not the 'virile' style, he could represent himself as the female partner, according to that ancient Scriptural tradition derived from the biblical Song of Songs in which the human soul and the Church are figured as the Bride or beloved of Christ. As the erotic sphere had become theologized (whether for the purposes of desecration or to render human love sacramental), so the religious sphere becomes sexualized. Such trans-sexual identification did not call for a revision of misogynistic attitudes: on the contrary, if humanity stood as female to God's male, that was because human nature incorporated all those defects Genesis and Christian tradition visited on woman: inferiority, fickleness, curiosity, and the covert itch for supremacy. There are arresting similarities between certain Divine Poems and the more salacious of his earlier erotica. The incongruous holy whore of Holy Sonnet XVIII exhibits a promiscuous ecumenism:

> Betray kind husband thy spouse to our sights,
> And let myne amorous soule court thy mild Dove,
> Who is most trew, and pleasing to thee, then
> When she'is embrac'd and open to most men.

(ll. 11–14)

Here the persona appears as one of many males competing for access to the Holy Spirit's sexual favours. In Sonnet XIV he presents himself as a feminine vessel soliciting a 'holy rape' by the Almighty. The call for violent penetration and possession, common to mystical and ecstatic visions of love like that of St Teresa, portrayed by Bernini welcoming her orgasmic wound from the angel's dart, is forged anew in the furnace of Donne's sexual imagination. The ABBAABBA rhyme-scheme of the octave is an oral mimesis of the enclosed space of the city desirous of being stormed and entered:

> Batter my heart, three person'd God; for you
> As yet but knocke, breathe, shine, and seeke to mend;
> That I may rise, and stand, o'erthrow mee,'and bend
> Your force, to breake, blowe, burn and make me new.

> I, like an usurpt towne, to'another due,
> Labour to'admit you, but Oh, to no end,
> Reason your viceroy in mee, mee should defend,
> But is captiv'd, and proves weake or untrue.
> Yet dearely'I love you, 'and would be loved faine,
> But am betroth'd unto your enemie:
> Divorce mee,'untie, or breake that knot againe,
> Take mee to you, imprison mee, for I
> Except you'enthrall mee, never shall be free,
> Nor ever chast, except you ravish mee.

Fourteen verbs in the first quatrain, dominated by the command or demand of the initiating word, ' Batter', introduce us to a sphere of powerful emotional activity whose throes are contained within the city-walls of a rigorously observed metrical form. The second quatrain, with its dextrous allegorization of the trope of the besieged town, riven by internal strife, is more reflective, but, with the exclamatory 'Oh, to no end', continues the passionate momentum, which culminates in the climactic sexuality of the sestet. However, sexual connotation is present before the poem makes it explicit, for the besieged walled town was a familiar emblem of the desired womb or woman. Donne had exploited it in Elegie XX, ' Loves Warre':

> Only thou
> O fayr free Citty, maist thyselfe allowe
> To any one ...
>
> . . . .
>
> Here let me warr; in these armes let mee lye;
> Here let mee parlee, batter, bleede and dye ...

> (ll. 3–5, 29–30)

In the youthful Elegie, Donne imagines manning the city; in the Holy Sonnet, he relishes the idea of being himself manned — perhaps one should say, Godded — by force. The final couplet, wittily calculated to shock and excite, glamorizes rape by raising it to the status of a spiritual principle. But, if the poem genders the persona feminine, its voice boasts a potent and imperious sonority which readers have learnt to identify with Donne's 'masculine, persuasive' language. In the ' Hymne to Christ, at the Authors last going into Germany' he would impersonate the tender and wistful manipulations of a jealous wife wooing God not the Father or Son but the Husband.

By a somersaulting paradox, the loss of his wife (commemorated explicitly in Holy Sonnet XVII) could be read as freeing him from being the husband of a mortal woman to become the 'wife' of an immortal Lover. The long-time browser amongst the pages of Donne's *Complete Poems* is so accustomed to such vagrancies that she or he accepts the exchange without a murmur: the extraordinary becomes a kind of norm. Looking up from the book, we are struck with the flatness of a consensus world where people walk on the solid earth of common sense rather than progressing by prodigious feats of vaulting up mountain sides of wit. Donne is known to have undergone profound mourning for his wife, who died on 15 August 1617, aged 33, after the birth of their twelfth child. He buried her at St Clement Dane's and, as Walton tells us, shortly thereafter preached a sermon in the church on the subject of Jeremiah's lamentation, 'Lo, I am the man that have seen affliction', in which he wept and sighed throughout the sermon so copiously as to stir the sympathies of the congregation, tearful in their pews. To dramatize his grief in the public eye was not to falsify it: for Donne, the theatrical production of emotion was its sincerest expression. He did not marry again.

Instead he struggled for clues to interpretation. What, he wondered, did God mean by inflicting the shock of this bruising intervention? The answer that dawned, though in essence conventional, was odd and startling in expression, because charged with imaginative cerebration and tending towards the absurdity of all excessive literality. Sonnet XVII begins as a moving valediction and tribute to his wife:

> Since she whom I lov'd hath payd her last debt
> To Nature, and to hers, and my good is dead,
> And her Soule early into heaven ravished,
> Wholly on heavenly things my mind is sett.
> Here the admyring her my mind did whett
> To seeke thee God; so streames do shew their head ...

His lost wife represents total value: 'my good'; a visual sign of the divine Source. But, in the course of the elegy, Ann is eclipsed behind the lonely, artful play her husband makes for the attentions of the amorous Deity, whose provocative 'tender jealousy' has 'ravished' her in order to ensure the exclusive affection of Donne himself. Perhaps we are wrong to say that Donne never married again. He merely signed his divorce-papers from natural allegiances, as in the 'Hymne to Christ, at the Authors last going into Germany', written under the same stress of loss in 1619, when, bidding for exclusive intimacy with Christ, he set out for the continent of death as to his own matrimonial consummation.

3

The Soul

Donne's journey toward ordination as a Church of England priest in 1615 was along the route of worldly ambition. He never wanted Holy Orders. He desired power, prestige, rank, and riches. King James, who had long warned him that secular promotion was not on offer, may have been rebuking his arrogant hunger by thus mortifying him, or he may have seen in Donne the makings of the spectacular preacher he would ultimately become. Coveting a worldly glory fitted to the brilliance of his pyrotechnic skills; conscientiously aware of his unfitness for Holy Orders and perhaps secretly afraid of committing a final trespass against his Roman Catholic roots, Donne held back until well into middle age. He was almost 43 when he finally yielded. With bizarre celerity he shot up the ladder of ecclesiastical preferment like a middle-aged infant prodigy, hurtling heavenwards in the pride of office with demonic energy: he was appointed Royal Chaplain almost immediately, and the disgusted University of Cambridge was forced by the King to confer upon him an honorary doctorate; in 1616 he was chosen divinity reader of Lincoln's Inn; in 1621 he was elected Dean of St Paul's, and at the time of his death was being considered for a Bishopric. Ironically, the 'worm' or 'nothing' who had solicited patronage from the great was now in a position to dispense influence and largesse; his charitable gifts were exemplary. Proud as St Paul in his status as 'chief of sinners' and nearly as eloquent, he discharged sermons from the pulpit at Whitehall or St Paul's in displays of oratorical thunder and lightning, ornate and Baroque in style and utterly galvanizing in the performance. Walton described the apocalyptic manner of his delivery, 'weeping sometimes for his Auditory, sometimes with them; always preaching to himself, like an Angel from a cloud' (Bald, 408). Donne saw his ordination as a coronation; from his cloud, the admonitory angel looked down with some satisfaction upon two kings humbled on their knees in God's (and Dr Donne's) presence. His subject was often himself: public self-flayings for present infirmities and past corruptions were conducted in a rhetoric which glorified through extravagant conceits what it also deplored, but could also hit the perfect note of simple admission: 'I impute nothing to another, that I confesse not of my selfe ...' (*Sermons*, iii. 182).

That confessional spirit, and his awareness of the ticklish nature of any human attempt at veracity, links the sermons with the devotional poetry, which, however, mostly predates Donne's ordination. The fact that the bulk of his religious poetry (the sonnet-sequence, 'La Corona', the 'Litanie', and many of his Holy Sonnets) was composed during the 'Mitcham' period, with its melancholia and directionlessness, thwarts any attempt to simplify Donne's life's work into the three phrases of juvenilia, love-poetry, and religious poetry. I have called this chapter 'The Soul' as against 'The Person' and 'The Male'. Although in a secular age the distinction may seem artificial, for Donne 'the soul' represented the immortal part of a person, and it remains in common usage to signify the deepest, most inward part of the self. The essence of a person's being, it is also the most alarmingly naked, and open to the eyes of God; when the flesh falls away, it is left, the centre of one's being, to answer at the final court of appeal. Donne was always, not just self-conscious, but soul-conscious. He knew that you could lose, relinquish, perjure, give, or animalize the soul. All human transactions affected it and might leave an indelible mark.

So the road to ordination had been, paradoxically, through a strife and soul-sifting which the worldliness of his drives and behaviour (persisting right up to ordination and beyond) only rendered more acute. The imperatives of the sermons are founded upon a deeper than average cognisance of inner foulness. They are also sharply aware of the mortality of the human animal. Though Donne enjoyed relative longevity, he knew the trauma of bouts of ill health which threatened his life. During a severe bout of relapsing fever in 1623, he wrote and published *Devotions upon Emergent Occasions and severall steps in my Sicknes*, a testament to that debatable honour which man has of 'being a *little world*, That he hath these *earthquakes* in him selfe, sodaine shakings; these *lightnings*, sodaine flashings; these *thunders*, sodaine noises ... *Eclypses* ... *Blazing stars* ... these *Rivers of blood*, sodaine red waters.'[1] The capacity of his consciousness to levitate above his sick-bed, focus and articulate his supine condition with panache, in letters, poems (such as the unforgettable 'Hymne to God my God in my sicknesse'), and sermons, is a tribute not only to the resolute clarity of his intellect but to his omnivorous curiosity about himself and his processes. He refused to be prostrated. Even his funerary monument defied the supine condition of the traditional recumbent posture; it rose in its shroud out of its urn, to stand with its Maker on Judgement Day. To write about abjectness was a device empowering him to take up his metaphorical bed and walk. And yet it cannot be denied that the older Donne had been battered by his conditions: illnesses were compounded by deaths — his wife, children, friends of a lifetime. In poems and sermons he responded with self-empowering wit to this dereliction. It was characteristic of his behaviour in affliction that, while he might retreat into temporary solitude, he would re-emerge to batter his own heart against the fortifications of God's obscurity.

The religious poetry and prose are lit up with apocalyptic horror. Time was running out. These writings communicate a state of emergency, in which the reader or hearer is given a lurid presentiment of the end of his personal world. In one sermon, he states his conclusion first, in case today turns out to be the Last Day and he has no time to finish it. Terror of Judgment electrifies the persona of the Holy Sonnets: 'What if this present were the worlds last night?' (Holy Sonnet XIII, l. 1); 'This is my playes last scene ...' (Holy Sonnet VI, l. 1). The elaborately wrought sermons with their cumbrously complex sentence-structures are hectic with teeming conceits. From their pages spill a pharmacopeia of medicines, whole zoos of animals, laboratories of scientific apparatus, and curiosities of all sorts: a ship's compass, a minute-glass, an hour-glass and a self-patented 'Secular Glass' composed of the two hemispheres of the world and filled with the cremated remains of the Creation; a Speculum which is the world, 'a glasse, in which we see God'; maps, giants, tapers, oak-ashes, worms, wombs, an arm that was lost in 'Europe and a leg that was lost in Africa or Asia scores of years between'. In a spectacular pre-enactment of the resurrection of the body, Donne imagines in vivid detail the forensic problems to be faced by God in reassembling the human bodies that have gone to jelly, been shot to pieces, passed through worms' digestive systems, crumbled into dust, and been tumbled into the sea — 'and still, still God knows in what *Cabinet* every *seed-Pearle* lies' (*Sermons*, viii. 98). The vile is made precious. Each decomposed cell of every putrefied believer is prized by God the Pathologist in the global mortuary. Nothing more plainly confirms the absurdity of Donne's God: and that he recognized him as absurd, without any nervous need to cover up for his extra-ordinary ways with misty generalizations. Where so many Anglican divines handed out a stale communion with a standardized God — old bread and tasteless wine — Donne took the scriptures with a radical and often bizarre literality which gave both novelty and substance to traditional ideas.

The famous 'tolling bell' sermon has a sombre magnificence which begins in the unlikely and grotesque fantasy of a coffined corpse listening in to the tolling of his own passing bell. Unwinding through serpentine puns and disturbing manipulations of the congregation's feelings, Donne moves to the immortal climax:

> No man is an *Iland*, intire of itself: every man is a peece of the *Continent*, a part of the *maine*; if a *Clod* bee washed away by the *Sea*, *Europe* is the Lesse, as well as if a *Promontorie* were, as well as if a *Mannor* of thy *friends*, or of *thine owne* were; any mans *death* diminishes *me*, because I am involved in *Mankinde*; And therefore never send to know for whom the *bell* tolls, it tolls for *thee*. (*Sermons*, vii. 369)

Ironically, all his life Donne had been, and remained, an island, cursed and blessed with singularity. Further, he had been an islander whose excursion to the Continent in 1619 was mytholo-gized in 'A Hymne to Christ': 'I sacrifice this Iland unto thee, | And all whom I lov'd there, and who lov'd mee' (ll. 9–10). The 'Iland' represents that 'I-land', the earthly sanctuary of 'I', the ego, which, in that moving valedictory, casts adrift into the stormy seas of self-annihilation which are the only route to Heaven. The rhetorical magnificence of the sermon derives from an imaginary abdication of the 'I-land', to incorporate the self in the panorama of a mortal world envisaged from the telescopic advantage of the pulpit as one mighty whole in which there are no distinctions of degree, and the clod of clay the sea erodes is neither more nor less significant than any other portion of the mainland. All are dust that must return to dust. The sermon is cunningly angled at the susceptibilities of the congregation. As the one body of Christ's church, the congregation represents an incorporation of many members, each of whom has however a natural partiality to his own 'mannor' (the soul's dwelling-place, or mansion, in the body). Rating our own residences highly, we naturally deplore their erosion or demolition above the tenements of our neighbours. Donne threatens ringingly the bland complacency of his hearers, who somehow imagine that they are less mortal than the people sitting next to them. His climax points the finger at each individually: 'it tolls for thee.' But Donne's self-reduction with the rest is neither humble nor self-abnegating: rather it occurs as an exalted act of transcendence, claiming the prophetic elevation of a God's-eye-view. His towering sense of self unwittingly delivers a homily against charity. Should we really 'never send to know for whom the bells tolls' but stay in and meditate our own mortality? His overbearing logic ('if ... because ... therefore') and the resonance of new-minted axioms forbid our dispute. The sermon is an authoritarian medium; Donne's more so than most.

Nevertheless, awareness of his own devious mental processes and their power to betray, confuse, and distract is a fascination of the sermons. One of the best examples occurs in the incomparable evocation of distractibility in a sermon of 1626:

> I throw my selfe downe in my chamber, and I call in, and invite God, and his Angels thither, and when they are there, I neglect God and his Angels for the noise of a Flie, for the ratling of a Coach, for the whining of a doore; I talke on, in the same posture of praying; Eyes lifted up; knees bowed downe, as though I prayed to God: and, if God or his Angels should aske me, when I thought last of God in that prayer, I cannot tell: Sometimes I finde that I had forgot what I was about, but when I began to forget it, I cannot tell. A memory of yesterdays pleasures, a feare of tomorrows dangers, a straw under my knees, a noise in mine eare, a light in mine eye, an anything, a nothing, a fancy, a Chimera in my braine, troubles me in my prayer. (*Sermons*, vii. 264–5).

Seriously self-mocking, this passage treats us to an intimate viewing of the all-too-human Doctor at his devotions. The vivid detail, auditory, visual, and tactile, together with mental digressions (memories, apprehensions, fantasies), builds up an inventory of vagaries familiar to any reader or hearer. With exasperated irony, Donne distinguishes between his outward observances (pious posture, holy mouthings) and the chronic triviality of the mental activities they cover. He makes a fool of himself. For God is not deceived. Indeed God is in the room with him; he has been literally called in by invitation, along with the angelic hosts. There they hover in their host's room, keeping company with the annoying fly, in the space between the door that whines and the window beyond which carriages rattle past. And Donne ignores the presence of his holy guest, madly preferring the fly, the straw, the odds and ends of his everyday world, and the flotsam of his mind. Without the sense of the literal presence of God within the room with the worshipper, the passage would be a witty and well-observed trifle. But God, as real a presence as the fly, is also the fly's competitor for the wandering mind of his priest. The shock of the illusion adds a gravity to the antics of the flighty mind at prayer. For issues of Eternal Life and Death hang upon the transaction. Like Faustus, Donne must make account of his private soul. Is it ultimately God's or the fly's? It can be no coincidence that the fly was the form in which a familiar spirit was supposed to manifest itself to the invocation of the black magician. If the world and the flesh invade the prayerful spirit, so does their indissoluble counterpart, the Devil.

Drawing on the Ignatian techniques of meditation in their passionate empathetic re-enactments of sacred events, the imaginative *imitatio Dei*, Donne's religious poems also participated in this life-and-death religious drama. God's reality is projected as immeasurably greater than that of the mundane world. The Crucifixion and the Last Judgement burst into vision in Donne's devotional poetry, mocking the worldly pursuits of men — the 'Pleasure or businesse' of 'Goodfriday 1613' (l. 7) — as time-wasting distractions, and dematerializing the landscape so that it faded into a merely emblematic backdrop. Techniques that in the love-poems contracted and decentred the world into the globe of an eye were now adapted to the collapsing of physical space into religious inner space: the telescopic reduction of the heavens by those like Galileo who 'Have found new sphears, and of new lands can write' is marginalized by the microcosmic eye's need for 'new seas' to wash its dry world with contrition (Holy Sonnet V, ll. 6–7). Time, like space, is attenuated or bent, whether to a momentary point crushed between past and future, 'Despaire behind, and death before' (Holy Sonnet I, l. 6) or refashioned into that cycle of recurrences which forms the round of the Church Year. In 'The Annuntiation and Passion', in which Mary's conception of Christ coincides with her son's death, 'this doubtfull day I Of feast or fast' (ll. 5–6), Donne's strained wit riddles on the paradox of a liturgical anniversary on which mechanical word-play grinds: 'Shee sees him nothing twice at once, who'is all' (l. 7). The sonnet-cycle, 'La Corona', also belongs to this round of liturgical time, in which formal and conventional prayers interweave with the collects and offices of the liturgy. The devotion of the Virgin Mary ('*Immensity cloysterd in thy deare wombe*' (Sonnet, II, l. 14; Sonnet III, l. 1)), and the rosary-form of the sequence reflect back to the Roman Catholic traditions of Donne's youth, and the cycle has a formal tranquillity absent from the more personal Holy Sonnets sequence.

Here, a major subject is despair. The only certainty is of the disgrace of the speaker's own unworthiness. The sonnet-sequence is founded upon conflict between faith in Christ's imputed Grace and the Calvinistic fear of his own innate infidelity. These poems, obedient to a rigid and concise verse-form, express explosive emotional states which charge the form with nervous excitability. The War in Heaven was a civil war. So also these sonnets each represent the internecine strife of a soul at war with itself. A frequently powerful octave tends to modulate into a minor key in the sestet, the transition marked perhaps by conjunctions or exclamations signifying a turn from or modification of the initial emotion: 'Onely . . .' (Holy Sonnet I), 'Yet . . .' (Holy Sonnets IV, XIV, XVI), 'But . . .' (Holy Sonnets V, VII, IX, XVIII), 'No, no . . .' (Holy Sonnet XIII). Louis Martz demonstrated the debt of Donne's Holy Sonnets to the meditative techniques of the Ignatian Spiritual Exercises: indeed, in three of the manuscripts they are entitled 'Holy Meditations'. These exercises aimed to focus the whole person in an imaginative development of a state of 'devotion' through which the soul passed to mystical union with Christ. A request for Grace preceded the 'composition of place, seeing the spot' where a sacred event had taken place, imagining oneself there as a participant; after analysis of this experience, a colloquy would conclude the process, in which the meditator would strive for understanding and enactment of the event. The traumatizing openings of some of the Holy Sonnets clearly reflect this tradition, along with the related visual analogues of Mannerist art, which portrayed the effects of the Passion or martyrs' deaths on forever-changed witnesses.

Sonnet VII takes us to the Last Judgement; Sonnet XIII both to the Last Day and the Crucifixion; Sonnet XI transports us to a place we think we recognize as Calvary:

> Spit in my face you Jewes, and pierce my side,
> Buffet, and scoffe, scourge, and crucifie mee,
> For I have sinn'd, and sinn'd, and onely hee,
> Who could do no iniquitie, hath dyed:
> But by my death can not be satisfied
> My sinnes, which passe the Jewes impiety:
> They kill'd once an inglorious man, but I
> Crucifie him daily, being now glorified.

(ll. 1–8)

An initial illusionism deceives us into accepting the speaker as Christ. But, if we have unwarily fallen into this trap, we should already by the end of line 2 have begun to question the sanity of the author, for what Christ ever cried out from his cross with this aggressive masochistic snarl? The six imperative verbs of violent solicitation should surely convince us that a madman has climbed up on the cross in place of the all-forgiving, all-atoning Saviour. And indeed a madman has. We begin to detect our mistake in line 3, when the subversive 'I' of the poem detaches himself from the *imitatio Christi*, and flagrant, repeated depravities ('sinn'd, and sinn'd') crowd in between the 'I' at the beginning of the line and the innocent 'hee' at its end. 'I' and 'hee' are not only distinct identities but opposites. The persona's histrionic call for punishment is an ironic admission of his complete incapacity to undertake the spiritual exercise of meditation. The *trompe l'œil* appearance of identification with Jesus only advertises his repellent unworthiness, indeed criminality. The disqualified candidate for stigmatization inscribes himself as in fact more 'Jewish' (in the racist and prejudicial sense) than the Jews, whom he invites to turn upon him as a worse crucifier, on the model of Paul's letter to the Hebrews, in which backsliders are denounced as those who 'crucify to themselves the Son of God afresh, and put him to an open shame' (6:6). To be cast off and cast away is the Holy Sonnets' primary fear. The turbulent voice of the octave, with its call to be spat upon and abused, articulates this fear of a God who may reject, curse, turn from him. Such exclusion would be worse than the physical and verbal abuse he stimulates his imagination to conjure, rather as the lash of the flagellant is anodyne to mental pain. But deeper undercurrents disturb the melodramatic device with psychological resonance, for it advertises the fact that the 'imitation of Christ' may be a dangerous spiritual exercise, tempting the meditator to an act of blasphemous usurpation. The 'I' of the sonnet has displaced and replaced the mild Christ of Calvary with an arrogant demonstration of its own unique iniquity: there is a kind of exaltation in the tone in which he claims to be more sinful than the Jews, who only killed (so far as they knew) an ordinary man, whereas he daily murders Christ Risen. In the sestet, attempt is made at resolution of this estrangement of 'I' from 'hee' through an ultimately conventional couplet-paradox which fails to convince the reader that the poem has done much more than end: 'God cloth'd himselfe in vile mans flesh, that so I Hee might be weake enough to suffer woe' (ll. 13–14).

In the sonnet sequence, Donne's habitual melancholy, ripening, has brought forth the black fruit of despair and self-division, which assumes a Faustian emergency status. Time is lacking. The very brevity of the sonnet-form reinforces the sense of abortiveness, through its profound compression of a mass of complex thought and feeling into the mere fourteen lines available. Dynamically stressed rhythms, changes of pitch, and rhetorical forcefulness (imperative verbs, rhetorical questions, exclamations, 'oh!' and 'ah!', repetitions, and adverbs connoting immediacy — 'now' and 'here') give the poems violent momentum and impact. In the first of the sonnets, mortality of the body wedges one kind of panic against another, desperation of spirit. Compared with the fanfare-blast of 'At the round earth's imagin'd corners' (Holy Sonnet VII) or the triumphal 'Death be not proud' (Holy Sonnet X), the sonnet's manner is restrained, and becomes more so. Even so, Donne's solicitations are rather demands than wooings:

> Thou hast made me, And shall thy worke decay?
> Repaire me now, for now mine end doth haste,
> I runne to death, and death meets me as fast,
> And all my pleasures are like yesterday;
> I dare not move my dimme eyes any way,
> Despaire behind, and death before doth cast
> Such terrour, and my feeble flesh doth waste
> By sinne in it, which it t'wards hell doth weigh:
> Onely thou art above, and when towards thee
> By thy leave I can looke, I rise againe;
> But our old subtle foe so tempteth me,
> That not one houre my selfe I can sustaine;
> Thy Grace may wing me to prevent his art,
> And thou like Adamant draw mine iron heart.

The first half line ('Thou hast made me') articulates an unquestioning faith from which rushes a question which breaks faith with it ('And shall thy worke decay?'). Panicking in the hiatus between hindsight and foresight, the persona seems to have no time to address his Maker with the respectful devotion for which he might have leisure if there were more than this brief span of fourteen lines in which to wrestle his soul from Hell to Heaven. It is as if the persona dwelt on the caesura between the first and second halves of the line, insecurely taking panic-stricken breath between

'Despaire behind' and 'death before'. In this immediate and peremptory crisis ('now ... now'), he sheers headlong against his will toward his enemy, who rushes to meet him as if charging backwards along the same line ('I runne to death, and death meets me as fast'). The chiastic form — I : death :: death : me — reinforces this impression of two-way motion which nightmarishly doubles the total velocity and the imminence of impact, as persona ('I') collides with personification ('death'). The drumroll of alliteration ('death ... death ... dimme ... despaire ... death ... feeble flesh'), linked by the panting breathings of what is for Donne an unusually paratactic structure (five 'ands' in the octave), builds to a crisis which suddenly and beautifully modulates in the sestet. 'Onely thou art above' is a statement of wistful faith, which, acknowledging the grip of 'our old subtle foe' (that is, God's and the speaker's), prepares the way for the profound and virtuoso paradox which concludes the poem in a newly introduced rhyme (EE): 'Thy Grace may wing me ...' This is persuasive precisely because it is conditional rather than assertive: it claims so little. Out of the impasse between God's 'can' and man's 'can't' proceeds the mediating 'may'. The hard heart, petrified to mineral inertia in the breast of the prostrate speaker weighed down by terminal illness and the equally terminal sin of despair, 'may' (or may not) be the iron to God's irresistible magnet.

Donne's Holy Sonnets claim helpless despair. Yet none reads as an effusion of a supine man. Listless, dead-eyed, and inarticulate, our despair normally retreats into a solitude traditionally symbolized as the 'hollow cave' in which Spenser's Despair lived his spectral half-life.[2] Donne's poems signal their active desperation, like the Psalmist, by challenges to God. In Sonnet II he demands to know, 'Why doth the devill then usurpe on mee? | Why doth he steal, nay ravish that's thy right?' (ll. 9–10). As Jacob wrestled with the Angel, and Moses in theophany traded words with the Almighty, so Donne lays siege to God's incoherence. In Sonnet IX, pointing out that subhuman beings cannot be damned, he wants to know, 'Alas, why should I bee? | Why ...?', only to flinch back at the opening of the sestet at the thought of his transgressive and impudent questions: 'But who am I, that dare dispute with thee | O God?' And indeed it is a good question. The 'I' of the Holy Sonnets suspects itself to be unpardonable precisely because it asserts itself as 'I'. It proclaims self-doubt and self-mortification with a fantastic arrogance, and its mode of cowering is a form of reckless display. The 'I' of these sonnets knows there are quieter, gentler routes to God but that it never will or can travel by them. For this 'I' is compulsive and cannot choose to be otherwise. Self-dramatizing, it seems to admire the effects it creates: to be conscious of an audience or reader. These poems give little impression of being private meditations, inward communings between the spirit and God. On the contrary, they seem designed to impress; and they do impress.

Yet they are raw with guilt and fear. Their shocking keenness comes from the marrow or guts, and their religious commitment is in no sense skin-deep. For the 'I' of the sonnets is conscious that, in the very moment and act of speech, that 'I' is betraying itself. Each speech-act is an act of pride. Each poem's theatrical and rhetorical splendour is a kind of delinquency which God, who sees all motives, will not be able to overlook. 'Oh, 'tis imposture all', fumed the cynic of 'Loves Alchymie' (l. 6). Something of the power of these sonnets derives from their consciousness of their wilful failure as acts of meditation. The volition of the worshipper is, he argues, corrupted and depraved. But the sonnets are themselves acts of will: Donne, unlike Herbert and Vaughan, is rarely capable of the poetry of mysticism, in which the ego is mercifully absolved and dissolved into the being of the other (though the Hymnes move in that direction). Since the will is depraved, each willed invocation of God's Grace is an act of perjury and blasphemy. The remorse Donne suffers in these poems is not only real, and realized on the page before us, but generated by the act of writing fallen meditations. No wonder, therefore, that his despair is absolutely dire; the pitch of the voice charged with vexed emotion. The sonnets themselves are feared to constitute symptoms of unforgivable sin.

At a third level of complexity, there is a rebellious streak running through the sequence which congratulates the writing 'I' on its apostasy. From early days he had been excited by heresy and aroused by blasphemy: it is the converse of his ricochet towards conservative and indeed reactionary Anglicanism as Dean of St Paul's. Just as the Donne of the erotic poems had traded insultingly on his image as careless philanderer, so in the Holy Sonnets he brags his worthlessness like a scoundrel's trophy. The black of his filthy spiritual condition is worn with a kind of exhibitionistic vanity: 'Oh my blacke Soule!', he exclaims in Sonnet IV, and 'blacke' (not of dirt but of penitence) becomes a rhyme-word in the sestet (l.

11), in which a palette of saving colours is produced to dye his 'red' blushing soul to 'white' (ll. 12, 14). In Sonnet IX he seeks to drown in tears of penitence 'my sinnes blacke memorie' (l. 12). Viewers of the melodrama of this colour-scheme, we rarely feel that we are witnessing a verbal process representative of the act of contrition, but rather a dizzy, dazzling reportage of the experience of life at the cliff-edge of disaster: a performance-art. Grace is not within reach while he continues to perform:

> Yet grace, if thou repent, thou canst not lacke;
> But who shall give thee that grace to beginne?

> (Sonnet IV, ll. 9–10)

The echo of Marlowe's Faustus' dialogue, within himself and between the Good and Evil Angels, is vivid:

> Accursed Faustus, where is mercy now?
> I do repent, and yet I do despair;
> Hell strives with grace for conquest in my breast ...[3]

Donne's struggle too is in some sense a staged event, and, since he is not prepared to abandon that stage, with its opportunities for self-magnification, he remains and will remain splayed in a cruciform double-bind. Repentance brings grace, by right: but only abdication of the territory of the self makes room for grace to steal in. If Donne cannot leave the stage where he parades his liability to damnation, he must remain in a condition antecedent to that of repentance. In 'This is my playes last scene' (Holy Sonnet VI), he expresses a Faustian sense of shock at the termination of the time allotted to his performance. The terrible face of the Judge almost before him, he mimes the uncoupling of the two parts of the human duality. Death will 'instantly unjoynt' body and soul, before which emergency all he can offer is the craftily casuistical hope in the sestet that his body will take all his hellbent sins down into the grave with it: a nonsense. Finally, he scrambles for the Book of Common Prayer and the hope that, if he renounces 'the world, the flesh, the devill' (l. 14), Christ's imputed merit will purify his unclean soul — after the play is over. The disquiet conscience which so unsettles these sonnets is mimed by their rhetorical dissemblings, tactics, sleights, and shifts; by the knowing, condoning, and congratulatory eye which he casts on his own tactics; by the rue of a moral vision which grieves for the complicity it parades. A more tender note does surface, as in the wistful and reflective prayer for time to repent in the sestet of the mighty Sonnet VII ('But let them sleep, Lord, and mee mourne a space ...' (l. 9)), with the partially comforted ironies of the final couplet. And in the last of the Holy Sonnets, regretting the perverse inconstancy that seemed the very foundation of his nature, his wry reprimand of his 'devout fitts' which 'come and go away I Like a fantastique Ague' (l. 12–13) solicits no applause.

Out of the violent strain and tension of Donne's maturity sprang a handful of spiritual testaments which count among the most precious of our inheritance. These include 'Goodfriday, 1613. Riding Westward' and three hymns, 'A Hymne to Christ, at the Authors last going into Germany' (which can be dated to his journey of 1619–20): 'A Hymne to God my God, in my sicknesse' (referring probably to his severe illness of 1623, not the terminal illness of 1630); and 'A Hymne to God the Father' (probably relating to the former illness). Because we can date these poems and supply some of the personal circumstances which generated them, the relation between the life and the work becomes at this point less hypothetical. The hymns were composed after Donne's ordination, along with at least two of the Holy Sonnets, XVII and XVIII. But 'Goodfriday, 1613' may be read as showing him riding towards that destiny, even in the midst of his flight from total commitment. The variant manuscript titles draw our attention to the highly personal nature of the writing, producing a work that was not just occasional but impulsive: 'Goodfriday I Made as I was Rideing westward, that daye'; 'Mr J Dunne goeinge from Sir H. G: on good fryday sent him back this Meditacion on the waye'. This spontaneity is oddly comparable with Wordsworth's account of the composition of 'Tintern Abbey' ('July 1798 ... I began it upon leaving Tintern, after crossing the Wye ... Not a line of it was altered, and not any part written down till I reached Bristol'. [4] If Wordsworth's leisurely, ambulant rhythms reflect his walking pace, Donne's pounding couplets beat out the thunder of horse-hooves. But spontaneity is all they have in common. Metaphysical and Romantic inhabit incompatible worlds, in which time and space intersect according to different laws. The ground under Wordsworth's feet is eternally rock-solid, the picturesque vista sacramental in its physical reality and unified by a Pantheistic spirit. The landscape over which Donne's horse gallops has no rock-solidity, for the physical world itself is a kind of dreamscape through which the transcendent spiritual world bursts with a violent, Baroque derangement of perspective and proportion. A personal journey can be a day out or a symbolic pilgrimage: or it can be both. Donne on his mundane way to Montgomery Castle travels a cosmic journey. Exiting both from linear time and the reassuring bearings of spatial norms, he finds himself entering the dimension of sacred time, which is cyclical, and sacred geography which superimposes an alternative set of compass bearings upon the familiar map. Sacred time and space are full of terror and awe. The traveller would really prefer to be elsewhere. But, although he would rather amble pleasantly to his self-indulgent destination, the destiny of Good Friday intervenes. The clock stops at the Crucifixion, and the entire universe is transformed in every dimension, save that the speaker is still proceeding westward:

> Pleasure or businesse, so, our Soules admit
> For their first mover, and are whirled by it.
> Hence, is't, that I am carried towards the West
> This day, when my Soules forme bends toward the East.

(ll. 7-10)

What does it mean, to be travelling westward? The speaker impelled like the rest of us by 'Pleasure or businesse' begins by brooding on a scientific proposition, comparing the soul with a planet whose natural motion carries it eastward but which is distracted in the opposite direction by the influence of the Primum Mobile. We may legitimately wonder, in this discursive opening (ll. 1-10), with its coolly intellectualizing tone, where are the horse and rider in all this speculation and of what relevance is the date 'Good Friday'? But the opening, which contemplates digression, is itself cannily digressive. It constitutes one of Donne's calculatedly oblique (not false) starts, yielding to a spectacular vision of the global map stretching before the traveller to a symbolic West (immemorially, sunset and mortality) and behind him to a spiritual East (the Holy Land and Calvary, the sunrise of Christ's atoning death). We, the readers, are free to view the fullness of that map: the speaker does not, will not, cannot. He can only bring himself to travel forward, without looking back, against the imperative bias of his soul. For what he intuits as lying behind him is a literally unbearable and unspeakable sight, which has an absolute claim upon him. The more he cannot look, the higher it soars; and the further he flinches from its directive to turn, the more uncannily real it becomes, both to his fleeing imagination and to the reader. But on one level we know there is nothing there but hallucination. Should the speaker rein in his horse and look back, he would certainly not see Christ Crucified on the horizon. He would see the prosaic road back to the home of his friend Goodyer in Warwickshire, just as before him he sees only the road to Montgomery Castle — the way to Wales, not the End of the World. But by its magnificent feat of *trompe l'œil*, the poem does convince us of the authoritative reality of that vision: a vision which is paradoxically all the more compelling for being *not seen*:

> Yet dare I'almost be glad, I do not see
> That spectacle of too much weight for mee.
> Who sees Gods face, that is selfe life, must dye;
> What a death were it then to see God dye?
> It made his owne Lieutenant Nature shrinke,
> It made his footstoole crack, and the Sunne winke.
> Could I behold those hands which span the Poles,
> And turne all spheares at one, peirc'd with those holes?
> Could I behold that endless height which is
> Zenith to us, and our Antipodes,
> Humbled below us? or that blood which is
> The seat of all our Soules, if not of his,
> Made durt of dust, or that flesh which was worne
> By God, for his apparell, rag'd, and torne?

(ll. 15–28)

A concentrated passion of religious awe is generated by the total focusing of imagination upon that which cannot be looked upon, theophany which is feared as terminal to the human participant. In plain words, he exclaims his simple inability to confront that world-shattering sight. Manner and syntax are almost childlike: a rare and moving abdication by Donne of the grand and tortuous style ('almost glad ... too much weight for mee ... It made ...'). Then a looming sense of presence begins to expand behind his back. The towering cross stretches beyond the dimensions of the earthly; beyond what our imaginations can reach to comprehend, if we view from a fixed point on earth, for 'hands which span the Poles, | And turne all spheares at once' (ll. 21–2) ('tune' for 'turne' in some readings) have to be viewed from outer space, or beyond, to be encompassed in one gaze — from which point the earth on which the figure rests must shrink to a dot and the traveller be invisible. But if we reinhabit the (non)viewpoint of the traveller, the horror of turning to view that revolutionary violation of human proportion becomes all too understandable. For the magnitude and power of the crucified figure as it extends beyond our ken into the reaches of space (which its hands personally created and control) intensifies the unbearable aspect of the wounding of these vulnerable palms, 'peirc'd with those holes' (l. 22). The self-questionings ('Could I ...? Could I ...?') seem uniquely private and as defenceless in their self-defendingness as the humane Saviour whom the fugitive is personally implicated in having pulled down from his gigantic elevation, 'Humbled' (l. 25) and 'Made durt of dust' (l. 27). In this challenge to spatial proportion, and the insistence on the astro-nomical dimensions of the beloved Saviour, the poem expresses a sense of threat to the cosmic structure itself, whose fabric desolidifies as the assassin flees his crime, too desperately contrite to be able to confront or express contrition. The insecure landscape, with the Passion building up towards the Pietà at its Eastern boundary (ll. 29–32), is numinous and spine-chillingly foreign. But a third section, drawing the poem back to the immediacy of the personal and present reality, mediates the Baroque threat:

> Though these things, as I ride, be from mine eye,
> They'are present yet unto my memory,
> For that looks towards them; and thou look'st towards mee,
> O Saviour, as thou hang'st upon the tree;
> I turn my backe to thee, but to receive
> Corrections, till thy mercies bid thee leave.
> O thinke mee worth thine anger, punish mee,
> Burne off my rusts, and my deformity,
> Restore thine Image, so much, by thy grace,
> That thou may'st know mee, and I'll turne my face.

(ll. 33–42)

The tone quietens reflectively, but the heart-shaken quality remains as the rider for the first time addresses the silent Christ, whose eyes he still cannot bear to meet but whose gaze the very nerves of his back seem to register (ll. 35–6). The poem's resolution offers the speaker's turned back to the burning restorative of those eye-beams and the renewal by Grace, issuing in a promise ('I'll turne my face') that cannot be fulfilled within the compass of the poem, which leaves the figure suspended in flight. The quivering tenderness and inwardness of the emotion, deriving from a quality of tone which cannot easily be analysed, rescues the poem from melodrama or unmodified display of ingenuity. Lit by the burnishing silence of Christ's sunrise and sunset (ll. 11–12), 'Goodfriday, 1613' reveals the resplendence of the paradox of God's love and power with an emotion which shakes the reader precisely because its expression is restrained. The Holy Sonnets had failed as meditations. But 'Goodfriday' in dramatizing the failure of meditation (the state of being unable because fearfully unworthy to look) succeeds.

In the hymns, Donne turned to music as the means by which language may attune the soul to its Maker's will. His raw, rough metrics had always been able to modulate into the composure required by song: Ferrabosco's 1609 musical setting of a stanza of 'The Expiration' in his *Ayres* was the first printing of any of the *Songs and Sonets*, followed by Corkine's setting of 'Breake of Day' in 1612. Walton records that Donne had his 'Hymne to God the Father'

> set to a most grave and solemn Tune, and ... often sung to the *Organ* by the *Choristers* of St *Pauls* Church, in his own hearing; especially at the Evening Service, and at his return from his Customary Devotions in that place, did occasionally say to a friend, *The words of this* Hymn *have restored to me the same thoughts of joy that possest my Soul in my sickness when I composed it.* (Bald, 442-3)

The hymnody of the sick-bed, that most private of testing-grounds, becomes a testament to a penultimate victory over mortality, which Donne makes public in its musical setting for organ and choir, elevating the grace he literally sweated for in his fever to a kind of higher narcissism, played back to him at evensong, amplified and ritualized. The hymn itself is a strange and rather wonderful weaving, or wreathing, of repetitions, over-burdened with the word 'sinne' (eight repetitions), which strives against the fourfold 'Wilt thou forgive ...?' Quibbling with his name (and, just possibly with his dead wife's, 'More', in the refrain), he apportions the entire rhyme-scheme between these two rhymes, 'done' and 'more', a riddling game of invariable repetitions that mimes the compulsion of sin to repeat itself, irrespective of good resolutions. The focus on the verb *to do* which derives from Donne's name sets his self-perpetuating misdoings in an ironic light, as a reluctant, ashamed boast, alongside the slippery quality of the doer. When God has

'done' forgiving, 'thou hast not done, I For, I have more'. The tone
is wry, regretful and confessional with a kind of uneasy levity, as if
to conceal a withholding. The last verse discloses in a surge of
candid grief what was being withheld:

> I have a sinne of feare, that when I have spunne
> My last thred, I shall perish on the shore;
> But sweare by thy selfe, that at my death thy sonne
> Shall shine as he shines now, and heretofore;
> And, having done that, Thou hast done,
> I feare no more.

The Sun who is the Son of God mitigates the severity of the Old Law
and reinterprets God's covenant with Abraham, made when
Abraham was lost in a horror of darkness (Gen. 15: 12–15). The
word 'shine' in the last stanza stands for the Atonement and expels
the corruption of the word 'sinne'. But it is less the theology than the
confession of buried fear that moves us, for it is not only a fear that is
deeply human (that at the last minute, weakened or crazed by
sickness, we shall despair) but a fear of being too human. To 'perish
on the shore' would be to experience a final forsakenness by God the
Father, who in his rigour and omniscience cannot stoop to gather the
merely and intractibly human soul to himself. That is why the poem
cries out for the mercy of a Mediator: Christ is the only way for God
to have done, that is, have Donne. But Donne, who will have (on a
literal level) 'no more' sins to forgive, will also have no more 'Donne'.
Personality, with all its conflicts and desires, will have been
abdicated, with the relinquishing of human allegiances.

All three hymns explore the journey into anonymity, measuring
their imagery and form to the process of attunement to this final
abandonment of self. The opening of 'Hymne to God my God, in
my sicknesse', with its unforgettable image of the watcher on the
eve of eternity readying himself to be 'made thy Musique' and
tuning 'the Instrument here at the dore' (l. 3–4), considers not only
the soul's preparation for death but also the function of the music of
the hymn he is now composing in achieving that finely wrought
state of preparedness. Here he is an active musician; there he will be
the passive music. The peaceful and contained gathering of the
dying self into a harmony of assent to the Creator does not deny the
trauma of the passage from voluble ego to assimilated soul. The
hymn goes on to lay out his dying body as an exploratory map,
where the strait/streights of fever (the central pun) is the para-

doxical route to final health. Just as a flat map betrays the shape of the globe by its representation on two dimensions, so the implication is that falsification may be the only way by which we can witness truth. The cartography is unstable. The dying poet surveys himself, both from the superior doctors' eye-view and from points within the latitude and longitude of the map, as a travelling explorer. He casts about him: 'Is the Pacifique Sea my home? Or are I The Easterne riches? Is *Jerusalem*?' (l. 16–17). The map, with its variant interpretations, is an area of uncertainty — a true Jacobean map, whose borders and measurements were always being shifted and redrawn in response to new information. In the penultimate stanza, a final bearing is given:

> We thinke that *Paradise* and *Calvarie*,
>> *Christs* Crosse, and *Adams* tree, stood in one place;
> Looke Lord, and find both *Adams* met in me;
>> As the first *Adams* sweat surrounds my face,
>> May the last *Adams* blood my soule embrace.

The map fades, as home is found and the poles of God and man meet in the travailing body that prays its way through the last strait ('Looke Lord ...'). The atoning blood delivers him from the unstable map, which represents himself, through assimilating him to a transcendent identity. The strait, when located, turns out to be the whole self.

Walton linked the bereft and searching tone of 'A Hymne to Christ, at the Authors last going into Germany' with Donne's loss of his wife, and this connection (true or not) reinforces something of the 'unsaid' quality of mourning and elegy, as well as its inwardness as it turns away from the mainland of the 'island' to put human bonds in the past: 'I sacrifice ... I ... all whom I lov'd there, and who lov'd mee' (ll. 9–10). Seeking the mutual tenderness and possessive fidelity of monogamous marriage with Christ, Donne must found his spiritual marriage upon loss and valediction. Its necessary condition is 'Divorce' (l. 25). Throughout his life, Donne had feared separation and rejection. They would leave him a stranded 'carcase', a 'nothing' in a world of alienation. In reading the three hymns, with their homesickness and their quality of tender yearning, I have sometimes allowed myself to reflect that, when traumatic loss came, in the death of his wife, it did not, after all, leave him entirely without bearings. There was somewhere to go: down into the earth which interred her remains. There is something of relief in the stanzas which record the peace of the thought of leaving the stage on which he had played so theatrical a part, with the anxious gratification to be derived from an audience of witnesses. Now he turns away from all eyes:

> As the trees sap doth seek the root below
> In winter, in my winter now I goe,
> Where none but thee, th'Eternall root
> Of true Love I may know.
>
> . . . .
>
> Churches are best for Prayer, that have least light:
> To see God only, I goe out of sight:
> And to scape stormy dayes, I chuse
> An Everlasting night.
>
> (ll. 13–16, 29–32)

The nature-image is as rare in Donne as is the quality of yearning mysticism it tenderly expresses. Here is surely a root from which grew the Metaphysical articulation by his friend George Herbert, and later by Henry Vaughan, of the idea of God as the lost home and natural source to which we long to return. In the conceit of the dark church of the final stanza, Donne movingly abandons the superficial light of day and the audience of eyes before whom he has constructed so spectacular a self: 'To see God only, I goe out of sight'. 'I chuse' is a conclusive and climactic self-assertion. But it asserts his abdication. There is a kind of terrible safety in the choice, and an intense sense of mystery. The poem's determination upon the journey underground to the root of love (implying eternal union) and into the embrace of the darkness proposes a sacramentally suicidal 'I'. It does not precisely predict that 'I' will have no further part to play; rather that we, the readers, will no longer be permitted to view it. 'I' will have no further textual existence and, however we strain our eyes, we shall never again catch sight of him.

However, Donne had a Lazarus-knack of surviving apparently terminal illness and returning from an ill-omened journey not only unscathed but in improved health and spirits, as he did from his embassy to Germany with Viscount Doncaster in 1620. With the greatest vigour, he began to preach again, announcing as his first subject a series of sermons reconciling contradictory passages in the

Bible. With grisly relish, he described the decay and decomposition of the human corpse; when he judged that the congregation had been reduced to a sufficient state of nausea, he sprang the resurrection on them, triumphantly. There seemed no end to him.

Notes

CHAPTER 1. THE PERSON

1. Thomas Carew, 'An Elegie', 11. 27, 49–50, in *Donne: Poetical Works*, ed. H. J. C. Grierson (Oxford, 1929; repr. 1979), 347.

2. T. S. Eliot, 'The Metaphysical Poets' (1921), in *Casebook*, 107.

3. *Biathanatos*, ed. M. Rudick and M. P. Battin (New York and London, 1982), 39.

4. Sir R. Baker, *Chronicles* (1st edn., 1643), pt. II, 156.

5. D. Parker, *John Donne and his World* (London, 1975), 39.

6. H. Gardner (ed.), *John Donne: The Elegies and Songs and Sonets* (Oxford, 1965), xxxix.

7. Letter to Robert Ker, in Bald, 7.

8. Michel de Montaigne, *Essays*, ed. J. M. Cohen (Harmondsworth, 1958), 348. 258.

9. Francis Bacon, *The 'Novum Organum Scientiarum'*, trans. and ed. Dr Shaw (London, 1880), 7.

10. Montaigne, 'On Experience', in *Essays*, 347.

11. John Milton, *Areopagitica*, in *Complete Prose Works*, ed. Ernest Sirluck (Harvard, Mass., 1959), 515.

12. Dante, *Purgatorio*, IV, 40.

13. See Gardner (ed.), *The Elegies and Songs and Sonets*, 197.

CHAPTER 2. THE MALE

1. Thomas Carew, 'An Elegie, II, 37–9, in *Donne: Poetical Works*, ed. H. J. C. Grierson (Oxford, 1979), 347.

2. John Milton, *Paradise Lost*, IV, 296–8.

3. G. Parfitt, *John Donne: A Literary Life* (Basingstoke and London, 1989), 79.

4. *Asclepius*, III. 21, in *The Hermetica*, ed. W. Scott (Oxford, 1924), 355.

CHAPTER 3. THE SOUL

1. *Devotions upon Emergent Occasions*, ed. J. Sparrow (Cambridge, 1923), 1–2.

2. Edmund Spenser, *The Faerie Queene*, I. ix, 33.

3. Christopher Marlowe, *Dr Faustus*, ed. J. D. Jump (Manchester, 1962) scene xviii, II. 70–2.

4. William Wordsworth and Samuel Taylor Coleridge, *Lyrical Ballads*, ed. R. L. Brett and A. R. Jones (London, 1963), 296n.

Select Bibliography

WORKS BY JOHN DONNE

Donne: Poetical Works, ed. H. J. C. Grierson (Oxford, 1929; repr. 1979).
John Donne: The Elegies and Songs and Sonets, ed. H. Gardner (Oxford, 1965).
John Donne: The Divine Poems, ed. H. Gardner (Oxford, 1952; repr. 1978).
The Life and Letters of John Donne, ed. E. Grosse, 2 vols. (London, 1899).
The Sermons of John Donne, ed. G. R. Potter and E. M. Simpson, 10 vols. (Berkeley and Los Angeles, Calif., 1953–62).
Biathanatos, ed. M. Rudick and M. P. Battin (New York and London, 1982).
Devotions upon Emergent Occasions, ed. J. Sparrow (Cambridge, 1923).

BIOGRAPHICAL AND CRITICAL STUDIES

Alvarez, A., *The School of Donne* (New York, 1967). A perceptive study of the growth of a tradition, taking up Eliot's and Grierson's concept of a Metaphysical school of poetry deriving from Donne. (See under Lovelock, Julian).

Bald, R. C., *John Donne: A Life* (Oxford, 1970). Still the definitive biography of Donne, at once readable and reliable, methodical in its scholarliness, ample in detail and prudent in evaluation. Its liveliness is achieved through generous quotation from Donne's own writings, allowing him to speak for himself.

Bloom, H. (ed.), *John Donne and the Seventeenth Century Metaphysical Poets* (New York, New Haven, and Philadelphia, 1986). Highbrow scholarship, not very readable, but a collection which will yield insights to the patient reader.

Carey, J., *John Donne: Life, Mind and Art* (London, 1981). No reader of Donne should miss this scintillating engagement with the whole person, work and imagination of the poet. But the critic has far too much in common with Donne — e.g. his ardent and uncritical zest for his subject's aggressive machismo. But even Carey's false notes are instructive.

Cathcart, D., *Donne and the Poetry of Moral Argument* (Ann Arbor, Mich., 1975). A useful application of the Jesuit theory and practice of casuistry to the complexity and contradictory speaking voices of Donne's lyrics.

Doherty, T., *John Donne, Undone* (London and New York, 1986). A post-deconstructionist assault on the individualist and liberal humanist tradition of reading Donne. Strong on energy and ideas; rather self-excited and tending to wildly idiosyncratic readings of particular poems, notably its interpretation of the 'Valediction: forbidding mourning' as a genital extravaganza and 'The Flea' as a phallic telescope. Should not be missed.

Leishman, J. B., *The Monarch of Wit* (New York, 1951). Old war-horse, still worth browsing through for individual readings of Donne's poetry and general sense of style, though pompous and naïve in his theoretical assumptions.

Lovelock, J. (ed.), *Donne's 'Songs and Sonets': A Casebook* (London and Basingstoke, 1973). Helpful volume, reprinting a selection of criticism from the seventeenth to the twentieth century, including the relevant part of T. S. Eliot's seminal essay, 'The Metaphysical Poets'.

Martz, L. L., *The Poetry of Meditation* (New Haven, Conn., 1954). This book remains indispensable to reading of the Metaphysical religious poetry, which it sets in the tradition of Ignatian meditative theory and exercises.

Parfitt, G., *John Donne: A Literary Life* (Basingstoke and London, 1989). A very useful, clear and sympathetic introduction to the relationship between the life and the work, divided into three phases, with Donne's marriage in 1601 and his ordination in 1615 as turning-points. The book is written in the light of post-deconstructionist awareness of the textual and historical matrix in which Donne wrote; but it is readable and jargon-free.

Parker, D., *John Donne and his World* (London, 1975). A pleasantly pictorial and amiably inaccurate wander through the life and works. His biographical readings of the poems are object-lessons in how to confuse art with life.

Partridge, A. C., *John Donne: Language and Style* (London, 1973). Dullish reading, certainly, but still a formidably useful encyclopaedia of information about Donne's rhetoric, metrics, lexis, grammar — fundamentals on which modern criticism is less well-informed than previous generations of readers.

Roston, M., *The Soul of Wit: A Study of John Donne* (Oxford, 1974). A rich treasure-trove of ideas drawn from the theory and practice of the visual arts, it relates *trompe l'œil* techniques of Baroque and Mannerism to Donne's poetic methods in poetry and prose. Highly recommended, because the application of Mannerist vision and values to a literary art-form is so skilfully and illuminatingly done.

Sinfield, A., *Literature in Protestant England, 1560–1660* (Princeton, NJ, 1983). A post-modernist account which emphasizes Donne's relationship to contemporary culture and society, its materialist approach makes a useful foil to the individualism of Carey (see above).

Smith, A. J. (ed.), *John Donne: The Critical Heritage* (London and Boston, Mass., 1975). An essential companion to Donne's work, a source-book whose excerpts from books, letters, and articles from the seventeenth century to the end of the nineteenth century allow the reader to follow the drama of Donne's changing reputation, plunging wildly in the eighteenth century. Ends just before Donne's restoration to the canon. Includes the fascinating pieces by Dryden and Dr Johnson.

Stein, A., *John Donne's Lyrics: The Eloquence of Action* (New York, 1980). Sophisticated and energetic wrestle with the structure of Donne's poems; close readings; sense of history; male-centred.

Summers, C. J. and Pebworth, T.-L. (eds.), *'Bright Shoots of Everlastingness'* (Columbia, Miss., 1987). A collection of scholarly essays, chiefly of the worthy-but-dreary school. M. Thomas Hester's reflections on the dubiety of the self in 'Re-signing of the Self: Donne's "As due by many titles"' makes a good case for the sonnet as a self-reflexive examination of the problematic character of the religious lyric.

Zander, W., *The Poetry of John Donne: Literature and Culture in the Elizabethan and Jacobean Period* (Brighton, 1982). A useful antidote to the 'individualist' approach, which seeks to set Donne's work in a historical context.

BACKGROUND READING

Bacon, FRANCIS, The *'Novum Organum Scientiarum'*, trans. and ed. Dr Shaw (London, 1880).

Barber, C., *Early Modern English* (London, 1976).

Chadwick, O., *The Reformation* (Pelican History of the Church, 3; Harmondsworth, 1972).

Crombie, A. C., *Augustine to Galileo: Science in the Later Middle Ages and Early Modern Times. XIII-XVII Centuries*, 2 vols (London, 1961).

James I and VI, King of England. *Basilikon Doron*, in *The Political Works*, intro. C. H. McIlwain (1616 reprint; Cambridge, Mass., 1918).

Lear, J., *Kepler's Dream*, with full text, trans. P. F. Kirkwood (Berkeley and Los Angeles, Calif., 1965).

Lovejoy, A. O., *The Great Chain of Being: A Study of the History of an Idea* (New York, 1936, repr. 1960).

Luther, MARTIN, and Erasmus DESIDERIUS, *Luther and Erasmus: Free Will and Salvation*, trans. and ed. E. G. Rupp and A. N. Marlow (London, 1969).

Montaigne, MICHEL DE, Essays, trans. J. M. Cohen (Harmondsworth, 1958).

Puttenham, GEORGE, *The Arte of English Poesie*, ed. G. D. Willock and A. Walker (Cambridge, 1936).

Southwell, R., *A Humble Supplication to her Maiestie*, ed. R. C. Bald (Cambridge, 1953).

Strong, R., *The Renaissance Garden in England* (London, 1979).

Wiley, M. L., *The Subtle Knot: Creative Scepticism in Seventeenth Century England* (London, 1952).

Index

New and Forthcoming Titles in the New Series of
WRITERS AND THEIR WORK

PUBLISHED

Title	Author
John Clare	*John Lucas*
Joseph Conrad	*Cedric Watts*
John Donne	*Stevie Davies*
Doris Lessing	*Elizabeth Maslen*
Christopher Marlowe	*Thomas Healy*
Andrew Marvell	*Annabel Patterson*

IN PREPARATION

Title	Author
W.H. Auden	*Stan Smith*
Aphra Behn	*Sue Wiseman*
Angela Carter	*Lorna Sage*
Children's Literature	*Kimberley Reynolds*
Elizabeth Gaskell	*Kate Flint*
William Golding	*Kevin McCarron*
William Hazlitt	*J.B. Priestley; R.L. Brett (introduction by Michael Foot)*
George Herbert	*T.S. Eliot (introduction by Peter Porter)*
Henry James - The Later Novels	*Barbara Hardy*
James Joyce	*Steve Connor*
King Lear	*Terence Hawkes*
Sir Thomas Malory	*Catherine La Farge*
Ian McEwan	*Kiernan Ryan*
Walter Pater	*Laurel Brake*
Jean Rhys	*Helen Carr*
The Sensation Novel	*Lyn Pykett*
Edmund Spencer	*Colin Burrow*
J.R.R. Tolkien	*Charles Moseley*
Mary Wollstonecraft	*Jane Moore*
Virginia Woolf	*Laura Marcus*
William Wordsworth	*Jonathan Bate*

For a complete catalogue of new and forthcoming titles in WRITERS AND THEIR WORK - NEW SERIES and for a stocklist of the original series titles still available please contact:
The Publicity Department (WTW) Northcote House Publishers Ltd., Plymbridge House, Estover, Plymouth, Devon PL6 7PZ. United Kingdom. Tel: 0752 735251 / 695745 Fax: 0752 695699